PRAISE FOR
IT'S ALL ABOUT THE PEOPLE

Having had the opportunity to work with Pat Kunz and the company he led for many years, I was delighted to learn that he was willing to share his secrets to success. Now, I'm even more pleased to endorse his book. Successful leadership is never easy … but when Pat made people, teamwork, and a total commitment to excellence his full focus and goal, the results were outstanding. I was fortunate enough to watch the company explode with success, so I enthusiastically recommend the advice he shares.

—Mary Scott Nabers, CEO, Strategic Partnerships, Inc.

Patrick Kunz gets it right with his book, *It's All about the People*. Companies are built into communities by the people working together to accomplish common goals. Truly, it has always been and always will be about the people and our ability as leaders to lead with empathy.

—Kathleen Quinn Votaw, founder and CEO, Talent Trust Inc.

Leadership is about people—listening to everyone on your team, understanding the culture of your team, and guiding your entire team to work together for a common goal. Pat Kunz understands leadership well and clearly provides a blueprint for leadership success in *It's All about the People*.

—Hon. R. Wayne Smith, PE, FNSPE, former state representative of Texas

Having met with Pat on a monthly basis for over five years, no CEO I've ever met cared more for people—and especially his employees. Pat had a strategic and sometimes stressful process for making key decisions that led to tremendous growth while maintaining a great culture. This book provides vital insights to leading and growing your organization in an efficient and powerful way that puts people first.

—Dennis Howard, CEO, Vistage Chair

IT'S ALL ABOUT THE PEOPLE

PATRICK L. KUNZ

IT'S ALL ABOUT
THE PEOPLE

The Executive's Guide to Success

in Leadership and Life

 *Advantage* | Books

Published by Advantage, Charleston, South Carolina.
Member of Advantage Media.

ADVANTAGE is a registered trademark, and the Advantage colophon is a trademark of Advantage Media Group, Inc.

Printed in the United States of America.

10 9 8 7 6 5 4 3 2 1

ISBN: 978-1-64225-404-4 (Paperback)
ISBN: 978-1-64225-442-6 (eBook)

LCCN: 2022919011

Cover design by Matthew Morse.

This publication is designed to provide accurate and authoritative information in regard to the subject matter covered. It is sold with the understanding that the publisher is not engaged in rendering legal, accounting, or other professional services. If legal advice or other expert assistance is required, the services of a competent professional person should be sought.

Advantage Media helps busy entrepreneurs, CEOs, and leaders write and publish a book to grow their business and become the authority in their field. Advantage authors comprise an exclusive community of industry professionals, idea-makers, and thought leaders. Do you have a book idea or manuscript for consideration? We would love to hear from you at **AdvantageMedia.com**.

CONTENTS

ABOUT THE AUTHOR

PATRICK L. KUNZ is a husband, father, and leadership mentor and the former president of Halff Associates, a thousand-person engineering and architecture firm based in the Dallas, Texas, area. Pat is a 1979 civil engineering graduate of Texas A&M.

During his forty-year career at Halff, including twenty-three years on the management team (sixteen years as chief operating officer and seven years as president), the company experienced substantial growth, expanding from forty to one-thousand-plus people. During this time, the company expanded its geographical reach from one office in Dallas to a firm of twenty-three offices in five states.

Pat was instrumental in driving growth, with a constant focus on growing revenue through both internal and external initiatives. Some notable accomplishments included adding key people throughout the firm to propel growth in existing and new business lines, as well as driving mergers and acquisitions to expand business in new markets.

A cornerstone of Pat's leadership focus was to achieve this growth while maintaining and building a people-centric culture of teamwork, autonomy, creative thinking, quality of service, and high integrity. Continuous unwavering attention on maintaining and building on these core values created a sense of ownership and teamwork. This resulted in a highly motivated team focused on growth and with an understanding that the growth of the firm would result in both career growth and financial rewards for all.

During Pat's leadership tenure, the firm was recognized as one of "the best firms to work for" by Zweig Group, the *Dallas Morning News* and the *Austin American-Statesman*. The firm was also recognized by the Southern Methodist University Cox School of Business as one of the top one hundred fastest-growing firms in the Dallas region—for multiple years—and by the *Dallas Business Journal* as a fast-growing Middle Market 50 company.

After years of watching the firm grow and leading change along the way, Pat retired, reconnected with family and friends, and began crafting this book about the lessons he has learned in life and business. His involvement in all facets of business during his forty-year career—marketing, financial, human resources, operations, etc.—has given Pat unparalleled insights into the business world to share. He has a desire to help people connect and understand their colleagues in the workplace while building strong, caring cultures that produce positive results, much of which showed on the annual financial statements.

It's the little things that matter. In the end, you might find that money can buy you experiences and maybe even a little happiness. But it can't buy you joy and fulfillment.

ACKNOWLEDGMENTS

THANK YOU TO a couple of people who are no longer with us, who taught me so much about life: my mom, Rita, and my brother-in-law, Calvin. Their lessons served me well in life and in leadership. Thanks to my brother, Dan, and sisters, Betty and Laverne, who have always been there. To the greatest mentor in my professional career, Dr. Albert H. Halff, for helping me understand that business is all about people. To my early mentor, Jose I. Novoa, the most creative man I have known. He taught me how to be an engineer and to think outside the box. To my coworker and good friend, Roman, who shared the leadership journey with me. To my coach, Dennis—without his encouragement, this book would never have happened.

And of course, thank you to my family. My children, Robert, Stephanie, and Jennifer, who have kept me grounded, young at heart, and in tune with future generations and have always supported me. My wife, Kathy, who has always been there throughout this journey. She helped to shape my thoughts and has been by my side for the past thirty-seven years.

Thank you to all of you.

INTRODUCTION

There comes a point in every leader's life when they step back and ask, "Was it really worth it?"

It often comes later in life, after they've made the money, reached financial stability, and achieved many goals in business. They look back at everything they accomplished and know they can retire comfortably, leaving the organization and the people within in good shape for the future.

Then that question really becomes, "But was I really successful? Was it all really worth it?"

For some people, the answer is yes. Yet for many, they look back on their lives with the realization that there's much more to it than financial rewards and achievements in business. *If they've been chasing results and living on the adrenaline of achievement, they might wake up one day and realize they're not happy—and maybe never have been truly happy.*

There's more to life than business success, and leaders need to understand that before they get burned out, discouraged, depressed, or just old and grumpy. I wrote this book to give back—to share lessons learned so that no matter what kind of person or leader you are or where you are in your journey, you will benefit.

You Can't Buy Peace

I reached the top step of my journey and asked myself if it was worth it. The answer is yes—I think it was. But I learned a lot of valuable lessons along the way. One of the most important lessons is this: *you can't buy inner peace*. Financial stability and business achievements cannot buy inner peace. This took me many years to learn. And it took several unexpected turns along the way for me to see it.

Leadership isn't for the faint of heart. Not everyone wants to make it to the top. But if you want to—be careful what you wish for—it's not as pretty as it looks. Business is constantly changing, the rules are constantly changing, and you're changing too. Who you were a decade ago isn't exactly who you are now, and who you are now won't exactly match your future self either.

After decades running a company, *I realized that making it to the top and making enough money to be financially stable weren't the answer*. Some people I talk with have a *specific number* in mind they want to reach. "If I make *X* dollars, I can retire and be happy," they say. But I'm here to tell you that even if you reach that goal, the money itself won't make you happy.

I led a company and achieved great returns, but eventually I discovered those achievements alone didn't satisfy me. I'm telling my story in hopes that you learn enough about leadership to help you align your work and life in ways that fulfill you in the end.

And the first step in this lifelong process is to ask yourself what makes you happy. How do you define success? Is it being a CEO? Or reaching a certain level of financial wealth?

My personal fulfillment in my leadership walk came from *people*, and from helping people grow. I believe there must be a human element to your leadership legacy that involves connecting with others and giving back to those who helped you achieve success.

The Driver and the Engine

Leaders need to possess a balance: you ***drive the business*** while ***showing empathy for the people*** within the business. Because after all, it's the people who are the engine of the business—and the engine needs a driver who knows where it is supposed to go.

People want to be heard and appreciated. They want to come to work and feel inspired! If you step back and think outside yourself, not only will people appreciate your leadership, but your organization will benefit as well.

> My personal fulfillment in my leadership walk came from ***people***, and from helping people grow.

> *People are the answer to everything.*

You'll read about many professional and personal challenges I faced throughout my leadership journey. Despite the challenges, I thank God often for all the good fortune he's given me. I thank him for family, friends, and the skills he gave me to be successful.

I want to tell you a story to help guide you to that end—to talk about some of the things I learned and that impacted my leadership vision—so you can find your passion, your purpose, your vision. It might also help you to find happiness and professional fulfillment earlier in life than I did. My goal is to give you some tips and lessons for leadership as well as for life.

I wrote this book in the hope that you could maybe take some of the lessons I learned along the way and use them to help you in your journey through life and leadership. I was really unaware of many of the lessons I learned until some pretty traumatic events occurred. I have also seen people—leaders who achieved great success in their careers—who climbed to the top of the mountain, yet they are very unhappy. I think that's because when they look back at what they achieved, it looks good and sounds good by the way society measures success, but it really did not fulfill their innermost goals in life. I think that I was headed for that end, had it not been for some challenging events in my life that caused me to pause and reflect on who I was and make some adjustments along the way. In my situation, I have also come to realize how fortunate I was, because the values of the founder and the leaders of the company I worked for were aligned with my core values. I think that many people aren't so lucky; they simply continue to work in an environment that is in fact inconsistent with who they are, and just keep doing what the company and society say they should do without ever asking the question, "When I am done, will I be able to look back and say I had success in the way that I define it?" Hopefully this book will help you understand this concept better, will compel you to take time to ponder it and make some adjustments along the way to ensure personal success and be a better leader.

CHAPTER 1

WHAT IS LEADERSHIP?

Knowing yourself is the beginning of all wisdom.
—ARISTOTLE

Passion. Purpose. Vision.

Great leaders *lead* people, *care* about people, and want to see people *grow*.

When I took over as chief operating officer of my company, I told myself to work hard to make it a better place to work. I committed myself to building a people-oriented culture of teamwork and collaboration. It took time, but we made it happen. We changed the workplace that had eroded into a self-based culture into one in which everyone respects and helps others.

People often have misconceptions about what makes an effective leader. Most of the time, effective leadership simply springs from the leaders themselves and their *personal values*.

I was committed to a people-oriented culture—that was my vision, *my passion*. I recognize and understand that now, but it took a lot of twists and turns for me to realize that.

Have you ever thought about how much you could have accomplished if you had demonstrated *your* passion earlier in your career? How much happier you would have been with the results of your work?

PASSION GIVES YOU PURPOSE AND LEADS TO VISION

Acknowledge your passion: One of the lessons I learned along the way is how important it is to understand and acknowledge what you are passionate about. How important it is to work on what that means to you and how it applies to your tasks and to those you serve as leader. As a leader, I believe it is vitally important to define for yourself what your *vision* is—in a way that others will understand, can find themselves in, and will ultimately follow. That is what leadership is all about: understanding your passion, finding that vision, articulating that vision clearly, and sticking to it, no matter what.

Keep in mind: Who you are as a leader ties back to who you are as a person. *What drives you? What do you care about? What are your goals?* Who you are at your core will influence all your decisions and actions. It requires time, experience, and deep reflection, but once you know who you are, you will better know how to lead. In my own experience, I came to realize that the main passion that drove me personally as a leader was caring about people.

What drives you?

Intentional Living

Good leaders don't become good leaders by accident.

They are *intentional* about life and business and what they want to achieve.

You must have a personal passion, purpose, and vision to reach true success. Too many times, leaders attend a leadership conference, grab ahold of the latest management trend—whatever it may be—and implement it as if it were some sort of recipe to follow. That will be effective to a certain level, but **unless there is personal buy-in and passion from the leader, reaching eventual success only by following an imported initiative is just not going to happen.** As a leader, you have to see and understand in your own mind, at a deep level, that what you are implementing resonates with who you really are as a person and, in turn, fits the people within your company and, of course, the company's own vision.

> I came to realize that the main passion that drove me personally as a leader was caring about people.

Strategic Planning

Taking the concept of personal passion, purpose, and vision a step further, let's discuss strategic planning. In developing the strategic plan for a company or for a team, the owner or leader *must be the visionary and own the plan.*

The most important part of what will make a strategic plan successful is to make sure you absolutely, 100 percent believe in it and are passionate about it. **You must have a clear vision and understanding of what the plan's long-term outcome will be** once its goals are achieved. You must also be able to clearly articulate how your partners and employees will benefit from reaching the goals of the strategic plan—and communicate that message consistently—over and over again.

VALUES THAT BECOME THE CORNERSTONE ...

In *The Four Obsessions of an Extraordinary Executive*, Patrick Lencioni outlines the importance of clarity-clear "rules," if you will, of how an organization's employees' behavior becomes an integral part of the plan.[1] These are the two or three **key values** that must be adhered to no matter what and become the cornerstone of a firm's culture. To do this effectively, a leader must **live** these values and ensure that these behaviors are adhered to. The only way for that to happen is if the leader is **personally passionate** about these values.

You cannot create a strategic plan with a vision and goals that will be highly successful across your company unless the above is true. Here are two essential reasons *(hint: you can't fake it, and a crisis will come and will test even the best plan)*:

1. People hear much more than just the words that come out of your mouth. You may think you can fake it, but you can't. You are not a salesperson selling a product to a short-term buyer. If your product (the plan) is not "sold" with passion and conviction, the buyer (your employee) eventually loses faith in the product (your plan). As you lead, the "buyer" will see you day after day and watch to see if what you are "selling" is true. You can't articulate a strategic plan with passion and credibility unless you truly *believe* in what you're sharing with your people.

---

1   Patrick Lencioni, *The Four Obsessions of an Extraordinary Executive* (San Francisco: John Wiley & Sons, Inc., 2000).

2. Your strategic plan, your vision, and your goals will all be tested when times get tough. It is in the most stressful times that we all revert to our own personal traits, values, and character. Or if we haven't made the effort to define our values firmly and extensively, we will let our emotions override our true values. If the business's strategic plan, vision, and goals don't align with your personal passion and values or haven't been well defined by either you or the business, it will show in times of crisis.

In the early leadership phase of my career as a project manager, a situation occurred that greatly affected my personal leadership journey.

WHEN THE REAL ME CAME OUT ...

I am a civil engineer by trade. Early in my career, I did civil engineering design for building-development projects. I felt, at the time, that I truly cared about my team. I had an engineer that I really valued, and I saw that she was very talented and had great potential. We were preparing the construction plans for a project for one of my developer clients. When the project was going well—in budget and on schedule with plenty of time to get the project done—I worked hard to take the time to teach and mentor her so she could grow in her career. But then the deadline got tight, we were out of time, and suddenly I was no longer so patient. When I tried to convey to my employee the pressure I was feeling to meet the client's demands, my facial expressions, tone and volume of voice, and choice of words were hostile. Was this the **real me** coming out in time of stress? If anything, it was certainly a time for deep reflection. I had been the recipient of the same treatment many times from my bosses when I was a young engineer in training. My harsh behavior was certainly not atypical in the business climate of the 1980s, so maybe I could justify my behavior as "that is just the way it is." Or could I? The problem with that justification was that my actions didn't fit my core value of treating people with respect, leaving me feeling awful after the incident, especially when I found her crying alone in her office because of how I had treated her. I then stepped back and tried to have a conversation with her about the events that led to my behavior, but it was too late—at that moment, I realized that I had completely deflated her confidence, and all she heard was that she was a failure. She ultimately left the company, and that was the last thing I wanted. So the end results of my actions were these: I felt terrible, production on the project did not speed up (and was probably slowed down), and I had lost a valuable employee. Had I made unreasonable and unrealistic demands of her? If I had handled my demands in another way, would she have stayed with the company? Taking care of the client, of course, had to be done—but the way I handled the situation with her, the way I conveyed what was needed and why it was needed, was anything *but* about developing and respecting people or caring about the team.

What drives you deep down is what will be revealed when you are under the most stress.

I didn't really understand who I was or what was most important to me at that point in my career—or how to relate that and the needs of the company to her. Instead, I was reacting to the stressors around me. While my core value was to treat people with respect, I had opted for a zero-sum game, subconsciously assuming that to meet my client's harsh demands, I had a right to treat my team harshly. Hence, I had accepted that being respectful to my clients and to my employees had to be mutually exclusive at times. Based on the results of this experience (feeling terrible, employee attrition), I knew my behavior had to be adjusted. Regardless of what had been modeled for me at times, treating people with respect meant treating **all** people with respect. With time and deep reflection, I came to understand that **employees may not always like what you have to say or do, but they will know whether you respect them or not.** At that time in my career, I was operating on a maladaptation of my core values, and change was needed.

"What drives *me*?" This is the piece that nobody talks about in the strategic planning process. You have to be able to answer that question. What drives you is ultimately what you are the most passionate about and thus where you will find the most success—or not, if your actions are not consistent with what is truly most important to you. Also, what drives you deep down is what will be revealed when you are under the most stress. Your thoughts and actions will be influenced by your emotions during those most stressful times, and your actions will reflect what is truly most important to you. You can't stop it; you can't hide it in those stressful situations. You may think you can, but you can't!

> **What drives you deep down is what will be revealed when you are under the most stress.**

Key Takeaways

- You must know what drives you and what your core values are. If you don't define and continuously evaluate your core values, stressful situations will define your core values for you.

- When it comes to core values, you can't fake it till you make it! Your employees will know whether you are walking the walk.

- Your core values must align with the company's core values or your leadership will be ineffective.

Call to Action

1. What drives me? Do the factors that drive me fall under the category of ego (power, approval, admiration, etc.), or do they fall under the category of passion?

2. How do I know?

3. How does this translate into the company's core values, vision statement, and mission statement? Are my core values consistent with those of the company?

4. On my leadership journey, do I take time for self-reflection? What adaptations or reaffirmations need to be made?

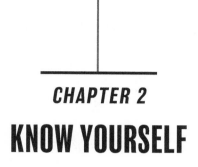

CHAPTER 2

KNOW YOURSELF

You can't be mature if you don't know yourself. Experiences,
failures, and reflection will bring you what you need.
—MAXIME LAGACÉ

Understanding who you are and what you are all about is vitally important. It's the only way to grasp what truly drives you. Why is it important to know what drives you? Reflection on your own personal experiences and how they shaped who you are and what is most important to you helps bring clarity when dealing with the challenges that a leader faces every day and in making the difficult decisions that a leader must make. To demonstrate the importance of self-reflection, let me give you a short autobiography of my life. Each "season" of my life will be followed by a reflection on self-discovery and the lessons I learned from that season of my life.

The House That Built Me

I grew up in Fredericksburg, a small town of about five thousand people in central Texas, north of San Antonio. My dad died of cancer when I was six years old, and that had a profound impact on my life. My mom never remarried; after my dad died, she spent the rest of her life committed to and doing an incredible job of raising four kids.

MOM

When I was born in 1957, my mom was thirty-eight years old. Later she developed diabetes—I think the stress of having a child so late in life triggered it. She didn't go to college; as a child, she grew up picking cotton. The days and years after my dad died had to be incredibly difficult for her, but somehow she picked up the pieces and made my life comfortable while I was growing up. I remember how she never missed a Sunday of going to church, and of course, I was there with her. I could be bitter and negative about the fact that I had no dad, but I also believe that's what gave me a lot of the traits that ultimately helped me succeed.

DAD

The only memory I have of my dad is of him sitting in a glider chair in the living room of our house watching a Boston Red Sox baseball game. Why, living in Texas, he was a Red Sox fan, I'll never know. Maybe because they were winners!

He got sick. I didn't know at the time why he was sick, but now I know he had cancer. Toward the end, he was in a veteran's hospital in nearby Kerrville. I wasn't allowed to go in and see him while he was there—I had to stay outside and play with my brother and sisters. I didn't have a clue what was going on. One afternoon my mother and oldest sister came home from the hospital, and they seemed to be very sad. My sister picked me up and took me in her arms. I remember crying in my sister's arms because Daddy was gone; I really had no idea what that meant. However, I remember it like it was yesterday; it's an incredibly vivid memory. Life went on for our family of five: my mom, my brother, my two sisters, and me.

MY MOM—NOW ALONE (WITH FOUR KIDS!)

My closest sibling was eleven at the time, my brother thirteen and my oldest sister seventeen. So my mother raised the family—hard to imagine a suddenly single mom raising two teenagers, a preteen and a six-year-old. She worked odd jobs and earned money babysitting for a time. When I was in high school, she took a job at the local hospital doing custodial work, cleaning hospital beds and hallways. She did the best she could. We didn't have much growing up. She was raising four kids and didn't have much money. Yet we never knew it, never longed for anything.

COHESIVE SUPPORT ...

When we were younger, my siblings and I would engage in the typical bickering that kids do, but nothing extreme. Once we became adults, I can't remember getting into one single argument with my brother or sisters. Ever. Maybe part of it is because, as a family, we all grew together to survive and make it. We were always supportive of one another. Based on what I see in my family contrasted with many other families, I think this cohesiveness is rare. But it began to shape my knowledge about how important *cohesive support* from the people around you is. I found out later how important it is in leadership as well.

HIGH SCHOOL FOOTBALL

I played football in high school, and that was a valuable experience and good training for life. However, not all valuable experiences are without pain. It taught me discipline and teamwork, but it also added to my awareness of the inherent unfairness of life. Of course, I knew that life could be unfair; after all, I had lost my dad at an early age. However, as painful as it was, losing my dad was essentially an existential crisis, beyond a child's understanding in so many ways. The unfairness of football was different—it taught me that no matter how hard I worked or how well I performed, there would be situations that are inherently unfair because of others (my fellow human beings). Football left a wound in my heart because I didn't have a dad—a dad who could help me, who could "kiss the coach's rear end" to make sure his kid was being taken care of. Wow, double whammy! No dad, and no fair treatment on the team due to no dad. To this day, I feel like I got the raw end of things. Some wounds never totally heal, but they can be the catalyst to the formation of stronger values and character. In my case, I think it was my experience with the football team, and others that were similar, that taught me to be more focused about the importance and value of empathy, appreciation, and perseverance. Scars and all, when I look back now, despite some tough memories, I am able to appreciate how *blessed* I was to have been raised in a town surrounded by *good people* who, for the most part, had a very positive impact on my life.

EARLY WORK

My oldest sister Betty is eleven years older than I am; she got married when I was twelve. She and her husband had about four hundred acres outside of Fredericksburg. I guess you would call it a farm and ranch. I spent a lot of time out there working on the farm, building fences, hauling hay. You name it, I did it.

My brother-in-law Calvin raised hogs, which is a lot of work. One of my jobs was to clean the farrowing house. That's a barn where a female pig can enter the barn in only one direction. All she can do is get in, lie down, and back out. It's built that way so when the mama pig has piglets, she can only lie down one way, which minimizes the possibility of lying on the little piglets. I had to clean it out every year after the farrowing season was over. It was one of my early, not-so-glamorous jobs.

Besides the work I did on Calvin's farm, I got another job at a typical Texas small-town dance hall, which was just down the road from where I grew up. My responsibilities included cleaning the restrooms, floors, tables, and parking lot after dances—another not-so-glamorous job. That's what I did to make a few bucks. It was our way of life.

THE EXTRAORDINARY INFLUENCE OF A MENTOR

Calvin became the most important male influence in my life after my dad passed away. I spent many days with him working on his farm. He was a gentle man, filled with high moral standards. He was unwavering in his core values, no matter the situation—and he always kept his calm when things went south. He saw the path forward with a positive view of the future, and he treated everyone with respect and compassion.

Calvin had a tremendous positive influence on my life, and the things I learned from him have served me well in dealing with the challenges I later faced as a leader and in my life. They are things such as remaining calm when adversity comes; looking for the positive in everything that happens; and being fair, honest, and respectful in how you treat others—always. He helped me realize life's too short to worry about the little things. And he taught me that life's not always fair—get over it; move forward. Calvin is indeed a big part of who I am.

LESSONS LEARNED

My mother did the best she could for our family after my dad passed, and certainly she, Betty and Calvin were always there for me. As I think back, I realize the early influence of these three people really made me who I am. I had to make my own life decisions, of course, but they helped form the deep values that have become the cornerstone of how I live my life.

> Life's not always fair—get over it; move forward.

1. *You're on your own.* I learned the value of independence from my mother and siblings. You've got to **make it on your own**, because you can't simply step back and rely on other people to do it for you. That realization caused me to become an independent thinker. You can flounder around in the negatives, but at the end of the day, shit happens. My family and I could have gotten caught up in the sadness of our lives after Daddy died and how unfair it was, but we didn't. My mother didn't, my brother and sisters didn't, and ultimately, I didn't either.

2. *Respect everyone.* I learned this from my mother, who treated everyone with respect. I learned to respect everyone at work. I worked some ugly, mundane jobs—I have never forgotten that; there's not a job that's beneath me. I'll go in the trenches and get things done. And because I did those jobs, I realized early that whether you're a janitor, administrative assistant, technician, or a kid right out of school—*you are an important part of the organization and deserve respect.* I respect everyone and everything they contribute.

3. *You will survive.* From the time my father died when I was six years old, I understood life would be full of losses and challenges. After he died, I watched my mother pick up the pieces and go on to live a good life and provide for her children. This taught me that no matter how hard things might be, you will survive. Losing a dad at a young age was one of the toughest curveballs that life could throw. Somehow my family and I picked up the pieces, survived, and in fact lived very successful lives. As I faced my own challenges, my family modeled for me how to deal with those difficulties. I saw Mom go on to handle hardship with grace, and for years I watched Betty and Calvin face their own challenges with strength and equanimity. The years I was growing up made me who I am. They gave me the confidence to know that when the curveballs come at me, if I just keep on swinging, I will hit my way out of this. Your life will be defined by how you react to those challenges in life and what you make of them. No challenge in business was ever more difficult to overcome than losing my dad.

My trials in life gave me the confidence to say, "No matter what happens, I'm going to keep going. I'm a survivor." But I've seen leaders who don't think that way. Maybe they haven't dealt with *a deep enough storm* in their lives yet.

What's happened in your life? **What has shaped you? Who has shaped you—as a person, as a leader?** Reflect, think, understand this about yourself and embrace it, because it will bring clarity to your life and make you a better leader. If you know who you are, what truly drives you, what your strengths are, what your weaknesses are—then what a better person and leader you will be.

4. ***Cohesiveness matters.*** My family's cohesive, consistent support taught me the importance of these elements—both in my personal life and as a business leader. The point is that ***all those interpersonal relationships will prepare you for who you are*** as a leader, even though you may not think so at the time. And you may not realize it until much later in life. Don't wait for something tragic to happen, or wait until it's too late, to reflect on who you are, where you come from, and what is most important to you. Your values and what you believe in as a person—and being consistent with those in your leadership role—will help you find success.

5. ***People won't always treat you fairly.*** We all bemoan the fact that others don't always treat us fairly in our personal lives or our business lives. Sometimes we are in a position to do something about that, but often we have no control over receiving unjust treatment. It may be extremely painful, it may leave a scar, but it will always be a growth opportunity. For instance, my experience with high school football taught me to think a lot more deeply about how my actions may affect others and to question whether I am treating others fairly. It taught me to be appreciative of those who provide me with positive support and to not take them for granted. It taught me that an unfair situation is just one battle; it is not the war. These difficult experiences can teach us perseverance, positioning us for later success in life.

6. ***Never underestimate the importance of a good mentor.*** Is there someone like Calvin in your life? Search out a good mentor if you don't have one. It can be a person, a book, a podcast or video—find them and use them for guidance and reinforcement. This is essential.

On a side note, I always like to think that everyone is a mentor in some facet. Sometimes they can even be a sort of "tor-mentor!" However, you can learn some important lessons from other people's negative actions, because you can witness the effects they have on people and the results they produce. This will give you the insight to steer your journey in another direction.

7. *A good work ethic.* I believe learning the value of hard work at a young age prepared me for success in later life. It taught me discipline, purpose and independence, but most of all it showed me that true inner satisfaction can only come from self-achievement.

Fredericksburg in My Rearview Mirror

... AND ON TO COLLEGE!

I was really into CB radios and eight-track tape players when I was in high school. My plan was to go to a technical school to become an electrical technician. One January evening, I was in our garage playing poker with my buddies. A couple of them said they were going to Texas A&M University, so I decided I wanted to go to A&M too.

I looked through the university catalog, and the closest thing to *electrical anything* I could find was electrical engineering. So I decided I was going to A&M to major in electrical engineering, whatever that was. I had to take all these entrance exams and tests. I scored well enough to get in—barely. I then had a session with an engineering school advisor. Once he looked at my math scores, which were very low—primarily because I hadn't taken higher-level math courses in high school; I never thought I would go to school to be an engineer!—he asked, "What the hell are you doing in engineering?" I wish I could go back and see him now and explain what the hell I was doing in engineering. Who doesn't love a good dose of poetic justice? However, while being predominantly left brained made me a good fit for engineering, subsequent exposure to introductory courses and a little more research led me to discover that civil engineering was a better fit for my interests and talents than electrical engineering. So I changed my major to civil engineering, and the rest is history.

Without a father in my childhood, we didn't take any trips or go on vacations, so going to College Station expanded my world immensely. It was during my college years that I also had a chance for the first time to experience the world outside of my little hometown, Fredericksburg.

LESSONS LEARNED

1. *Define yourself, or the world will do it for you:* I learned a lot from my circuitous route to becoming a civil engineer. Had I not believed in myself and what I was capable of, I would have dropped out of engineering based on the academic counselor's assessment of my skills. It doesn't mean we can't take others' judgments of ourselves under advisement, but we should never make a critical decision without doing a deep search of our own passions and what drives us and what we believe we are capable of.

2. *The world is a lot bigger than Fredericksburg, Texas:* Having never been out of Texas during my formative years, I learned during my college years that the world was quite large and much more diverse than I could ever have imagined.

I gained a new awareness of how limited my understanding of people and places was and that the learning was just beginning.

Working Nine to Five ...

THE CAREER BEGINS: MY FIRST JOB—AND FIRST TV!

After college I packed up everything I owned—mostly hand-me-down furniture—into the back of a friend's pickup truck and moved to Dallas to take my first job as an engineer for Dallas Power and Light.

I thought I had the world by the tail when I received my first paycheck and headed off to buy a brand-new TV. After all, cleaning hog pens and toilets had never paid this well. But I soon figured out that job wasn't right for me. Actual working hours were eight to "not a minute past five" (not

> We should never make a critical decision without doing a deep search of our own passions and what drives us and what we believe we are capable of.

nine to five like in the popular Dolly Parton song hitting the airwaves about the same time). One had to be careful to avoid being trampled by the stampede of employees heading to the elevators at exactly 5:00 p.m. Not 4:59 p.m. and not 5:01 p.m. I realize that most would think that this was a good thing, but I discovered that the stampede was a reflection of a work culture that did not suit me well. I was single at that point in my career, and being challenged and engaged with growth opportunity was more important to me than heading out the door at exactly 5:00 p.m. But the challenging growth opportunities were lacking. I started the process of seeking another position and in

February 1981 went to work for Halff Associates, Inc.—which was about a forty-person civil engineering firm at that time. During the interview process, I shared the story of being disillusioned with my first job because employees were never engaged or challenged enough to stay past 5:00 p.m. That turned out to be an auspicious comment! One of the managers who interviewed me shared later that he knew he had to hire me when he heard that story. The long hours were about to begin.

I was proud to be an engineer and thought I had a pretty good handle on life. I had no idea that the learning had only just begun! As a young engineer, my work consisted mainly of land development projects—often fun and creative but always with a deadline of "yesterday." I worked under the direction of senior engineers and leaders of the firm. The culture could be hostile at times due to the stressful nature of the budgets and the deadlines in a competitive industry with small profit margins. It was not unusual for most business climates to be a bit harsh during that era. At that time at our company, there was no human resources department, no core company values, no mission statement, and no leadership training. Leaders and managers, while often tremendously talented technically, were left to their own natural instincts when it came to managing others. Some fared better than others.

With a few years of experience, I became a project manager with my own team. Now the stress was not just limited to producing demanding, high-quality projects within budget but also managing clients, as well as managing and teaching a team of younger, inexperienced employees.

After sixteen years with the company, I was offered the position of chief operating officer, with the role of leading the "operations" of the firm. No one really knew what that meant, since there had never been a chief operating officer before. So I had to learn what that meant on my own—and define what that role was. It evolved into the role of working with the people of the firm to build a culture—to begin to define what behaviors were acceptable at the company. That had never really been done before. It also meant keeping a close eye on financial performance and guiding the firm to ensure we had adequate profits to compensate people well and to have enough left over to invest in growth opportunities.

Then at year thirty-two with the company, I became the president. To a large degree, I defined what that role should be—much the way I did for the chief operating officer role. In my role as president, I had the opportunity to build upon the many years of experiences and lessons that I learned along the way—the opportunity to lead and guide a successful firm into something even better and greater than it already was at the time. And hopefully to be able to achieve something that at some point in my life I could call "success." As you read the remaining chapters in this book, you will learn much more about that journey, the lessons learned, the challenges, the wins—and the losses. And hopefully you'll learn some things that will help along *your* journey.

LESSONS LEARNED

1. *Passion and purpose in work.* Though my first job landed me a good paycheck and the TV of my desires, it wasn't soul fulfilling. My first job taught me that I would never find passion in my career without challenges and projects that engaged me, even if that meant working long hours. I learned that you must have passion and purpose in your work to be fulfilled and to find success.

2. ***Once again, the learning is just beginning.*** The university engineering curriculum was so overwhelming and massive in volume that one tended to feel they surely have already learned what they needed to be successful in the work world. While that course work was fundamentally important, my job taught me that when it came to learning, it truly had just begun—and indeed would never end. I believe that having a deep passion for learning was one of the tools that I most needed to possess to be successful. The firm's founder, Dr. Halff, often said that you should never stop learning in life—and if you ever stopped learning, you were to come see him.

3. ***You will define who you are and where you are going.*** As you grow in your career and in your leadership role, no one will tell you exactly what needs to be done. You will have to define that for yourself. Know who you are, what is most important to you—so you will define a course of action where you can be driven to be successful—and how you define success.

Of course, we all started our careers at levels below where we are today. If you are a leader and forgot what that was like—what it was like starting out—it will be difficult for you to inspire your employees to follow your lead and work with passion for you and your team. I have seen leaders who treat their people very poorly. I have wondered if they ever tried to put themselves in another's shoes to think about what it's like to do that job day after day. *Do they care about those people at all? Do they have any respect for them as human beings?*

I was like that, too, to some extent, earlier in my career at times when I got lost in the stresses of the job.

However, over the years I learned that respecting other people—no matter what—is so important, and is in fact one of my core values.

The years teach much which the days never know.
—RALPH WALDO EMERSON

We Are Family

After about four years at Halff, my personal life began to change at a fast pace. I got married. My wife, Kathy, and I had three children, Robert, Stephanie and Jennifer, all now adults. In addition to all the leadership responsibilities I had moved into, I now had growing demands at home. My wife had also worked in consulting engineering prior to our first child being born. Back when our children were young, there was no remote work, childcare was not widely available, and technology was just coming on to the scene. Long work hours were the norm, and the prospect of balancing two demanding careers with children and no extended family help was daunting, so Kathy stayed home to raise the children.

From time to time, I hear that if you balance your life, you can "have it all." Whether this is true or not is very dependent on the definition of having it all. If your definition of having it all means that you never miss out on any significant career or family opportunities, than I do not believe that "having it all" is truly achievable. For instance, neither Kathy nor I had it all by this definition. She missed the perks that came with a career, and I missed some of my children's special times. The reality is that we make choices regarding what is most important to us. And you can "have it all," in that you can have all the things that are most important to you—and thus be personally fulfilled and happy. But choices must be made. I do think in the aggregate we did have one definition of having it all, because together we made it work and accepted that we both had to sacrifice something—but we kept the things that were truly most important to us. To make this happen, you have to know what is most important to you. *That is the recurring theme of this book—to know yourself, in your personal life as well as in your work life.* In this day and time, families can make it work in a multitude of ways, and it is imperative for companies to understand how they can support their employees with respect to family and work-life balance.

Previously, I talked about the high school football situation that taught me that when it comes to others, there would be times when I will have no control. Having three children brought that to a whole new level. While becoming a dad was and is one of the greatest experiences of my life, I have to admit (as would most parents, if they were truly honest), the actual experience of parenting is quite different from what we envision prior to parenthood. Our offspring come with their own prewired hard drive, and there is a limited amount of what we can do to mold the final product. Being a leader in the home is often much like being a leader in business. Mentoring, teaching, and setting the rules for your children is fundamentally necessary for your children and your home. It is also fundamentally necessary for a leader to do the same in a company so people can learn and grow in their careers and so that everyone in the company understands what behaviors are acceptable.

However, I also learned that for employees to be engaged and inspired in their work, they must have a certain amount of autonomy and flexibility to be able to bring their own ideas and creative thought to the table—just like children as they grow older. I learned that employees will react similarly to how our children react when they don't understand or agree with the rules or feel they are unclear—with some flexibility to be themselves—or when they believe that no one is helping them when they need it the most. You must have rules and policies to define what behaviors are acceptable; however, you must also be flexible and open to other people's thoughts, ideas, and priorities. It can be very frustrating when you think your objectives are so clear that you have the right answer—but no one will follow your lead! It is imperative that you, as a parent and a leader, understand and accept that you cannot control all outcomes and that you accept that others see the world differently and have different priorities than you do. It is difficult and challenging to find the right balance. The well-known serenity prayer is a great reminder to us that, in all facets of leadership, it is incumbent upon us to strive for the wisdom to know when we can and can't control a situation, as well as to know when to strive for acceptance. This can only be achieved through continuous open and honest dialogue. More on this in chapters to follow.

SUMMING IT UP—FOR ME, IT'S ALL ABOUT THE PEOPLE ...

A number of years ago, Kathy and I bought a modest lake house. It's comfortable and a great place for people to visit. That's probably what I love most about that house—it has become the gathering place for family and friends.

Memorial Day and Fourth of July celebrations with family and friends are what it's all about. Doing chores around the house while contemplating the meaning of life, so to speak, is a great pastime, but what I enjoy most is seeing other people enjoying their time at the lake. I can go fishing all day long by myself and have a good time, but what's really fun for me is when somebody else goes fishing with me. I put them on the fish, they catch them, and I can see and feel their excitement.

It's all about the people—whether at the lake, at home, or at work. Interaction with people, helping people grow, helping people enjoy and be excited about life: what's important to me in my personal life is what really drives me in business as well. Maybe that's where the inner peace comes from. My business life and personal life are different in many ways, yet they are the same in the most important aspect: to fulfill *my personal purpose of helping make people's lives better.* I didn't really realize this until late in my career and late in my leadership journey. I wonder how much more successful and happier I could have been in my journey if I had learned that earlier. Take some time to think about who you are: What's it all about for you?

> Take some time to think about who you are: What's it all about for you?

LESSONS LEARNED

- *Life is a balancing act.* I think of life as being like a tightrope walker in a circus. First, we struggle across the rope just trying to balance our own body weight. Then we add a ball. Now not only do we have to balance our own weight but also a ball. But here comes another ball, and another one, and another one. Before you know it, we're not only on the tightrope but also juggling at the same time, with many balls in the air. However, just like in a circus act, life experience, flexibility, and willingness to learn will help us keep our balance.

- *Did I mention that the learning is just beginning?* Often, the most difficult balancing act we all have to perform is to balance our work and our careers with our obligations to ourselves, our families, and others. None of us came with an instruction manual at birth, and the only way we learn these skills is through life experience, investing in ourselves, and having an open mind and a willingness to learn and adapt.

- *Know yourself; know what is most important to you.* The sooner you understand what's most important to you, the sooner you will find success in business and in life.

I hope my story will help you understand a bit more about who I am and how my experiences impacted my leadership journey. I also hope it drives the point home about how important it is to know yourself, who you are, and what drives you as a person.

I have emphasized how important it is to spend time in self-reflection, to know and understand yourself; however, it is equally important to also understand what we *don't* know about ourselves. These are our blind spots, and by definition, because we are blind to them, we cannot see them or identify them through self-reflection. It is only through others that we can learn about our blind spots. This is absolutely necessary to truly understand ourselves and to be able to be as effective as we can possibly be—in our personal lives and as a leader. I think this quote says it well:

You are not really grown up until you see
and understand your weaknesses.
—DR. T. P. CHIA

The key to overcoming our blind spots is to be willing to surround ourselves with people who will tell us what we don't necessarily want to hear about ourselves. I will expand on that in greater depth in subsequent chapters.

In summary, you must find what truly drives you, deep down. This is a recurring theme throughout the book. Whatever vision you have or whatever goal you have for your company, it must tie back to your passion somehow. If you can understand that and make it happen, then you can be much more effective at articulating to the people who work for you what you are trying to accomplish.

If I said, "I wanted to grow my company to be worth $100 million, and then I sold it and made $100 million," that would never do it for me. I would argue it would never do it for most people. Most will find out later in life that even if they got that $100 million, they still wouldn't be satisfied. Financially secure, yes. But satisfied— not necessarily. Worse, they wouldn't understand why they weren't satisfied and what was missing. They never took the time to find out what really matters in life, what is of lasting value: family and friends, selfless acts of kindness, matters of faith.

It's only later in life that most people say there had to be more to it, and often it's too late to make a difference. I don't know how a person can truly and honestly reach inner peace and feel successful unless they come to a deeper understanding of what is most important to them in life.

Key Takeaways

- Your life experiences will have shaped who you are and will define what is important to you, what your core values are, and who you will be as a leader.

- Life and leadership are a balancing act requiring lifelong achieved skills.

- You can "have it all" if your definition of having it all means determining the things that are most important to you and making a plan for it, as well as accepting that choices and sacrifices must be made.

• Leadership requires continuous learning.

Call to Action

1. *Spend some time in self-reflection—what's your life story?* What experience happened in life that shaped you? What effect did your mentors (or tormentors) have on your ability to lead? How do you define yourself? How do you let others define you?

2. *Define what your definition of work-life balance is.* What sacrifices are you willing to make to achieve your definition of work-life balance?

CHAPTER 3

LESSONS LEARNED FROM A SUCCESSION OF LEADERS

Succession is a moment when we are wise to walk with others, learning from their successes and failures.
—PETER GREER AND DOUG FAGERSTROM

The Founder—"Grow the Company so People Can Grow"

After my first brief stint at Dallas Power and Light, I went to work for Halff. The president and founder of our firm, Dr. Albert Halff, stepped down from his position as president about the time I started work. He had great passion for people and was driven by building a culture in which people could grow in their careers. He believed in only hiring people right out of school, teaching them, and providing them an opportunity to build their careers—and subsequently working their entire careers at his firm.

Dr. Halff's philosophy was, "Grow the company so people can grow." During Dr. Halff's long tenure, the organization's culture evolved into these five characteristics:

1. People: The leadership believes each employee has a role and a responsibility to deliver quality work to clients.

2. Autonomy: While leadership is involved and accessible, every opportunity is given to each employee to be innovative and to grow and think outside the box.

3. Teamwork: This is a place where people collaborate rather than compete.

4. Integrity: No cutting corners. Success is achieved by doing the right thing.

5. Quality: Quality is the cornerstone.

Leadership Successors

After Dr. Halff stepped down, he selected a president who had that same passion and vision. He was a strong-willed man who had worked his way from an entry-level surveyor to become the president of the firm. He was a brilliant engineer—the most creative, innovative thinker I have ever known. However, *he had little tolerance for poor-quality work and an underlying blind spot of a lack of empathy*. He cared about people, yet his relentless desire to provide a very high quality of engineering services sometimes caused him to not be so positive when working with people. In his mind it was all about right or wrong, and sometimes he had little ability to see things from the perspective of others. As I said, he was the most brilliant, creative engineer I have known. I can't help but wonder, if he had really understood himself, if he had really understood how brilliant he was, how things could have been so much different. How wonderful could it have been if he had understood that and been able to invest more time in teaching others, rather than expecting others to be his intellectual equivalent. I believe this is also the reason he tended to become aggressive when people didn't agree with him, see things from his perspective, or see complex issues as clearly as he did. While it was not this leader's intent, this approach caused people to avoid him or capitulate to his wishes, no matter the consequences. I felt it stifled creative thinking when it came to running the business, and it diminished our ability to achieve the level of growth we could have had.

The leaders that followed Dr. Halff also tended to be risk averse when it came to investing in building the business. All the leadership talked about wanting to grow. But when push came to shove and growth required investment, the leaders of the firm found it very difficult to take the risk. We often talked about wanting to consider mergers and acquisitions. After about the third time of pursuing an acquisition and seeing the opportunity die due to analysis paralysis— or in other words, asking questions, questions, and more questions until it finally died—I came to understand that the leadership's aversion to risk was greater than its desire to grow. This aversion to risk ultimately caused us to back away from closing any deals. Leadership at that time had lived through the economic recession of the late 1980s. Those days during that recession were uncharted waters for the company, which had only experienced fast growth up until that point. To keep the company solvent, bonuses were eliminated for a time, and a reduction in staff was required. Painful times for

> All the leadership talked about wanting to grow. But when push came to shove and growth required investment, the leaders of the firm found it very difficult to take the risk.

sure, affecting all. I believe some of the leaders of the firm never wanted to grow fast again because of the pain experienced during that time. One of the very important lessons that the management learned during that economic downturn was that no matter how much it was communicated to employees that bonuses were a function of the profits of the company, employees came to expect the bonuses no matter what. They based their mortgage payments, and their kids' school tuition, etc. on assuming that their bonuses would be maintained at an equal or greater level every year. With this lesson learned, we subsequently strived to set bonuses at a rate that could be maintained even during the downturns and adjusted by issuing a second "special bonus" in years of high profitability.

The aversion to risk coupled with strong personality traits that at times intimidated people were blind spots of the leaders that followed Dr. Halff, and the people around them were unwilling to point out those blind spots. I believe this stifled our ability to reach the level of growth we could have achieved.

Yet, ironically, from a people perspective, those leaders had the same desire Dr. Halff had: to help people grow in their careers; those leaders were deeply committed to the growth of the firm and the people within the firm. *However, the strong personalities, with little tolerance for error when people did things wrong, conflicted with those desires* and sometimes caused people to work in their own best interests to cover their own rear ends rather than work together with a sense of teamwork to do what was best for the firm.

There were brilliant leaders and people at the firm during that time, all of whom had good intentions, and the firm was successful. But I don't think it reached the level of growth it *could* have, nor was it as collaborative of a workplace as it could have been.

Those leaders that followed Dr. Halff were talented; however, sometimes they led with *a philosophy that the leader of the firm should make the decisions themselves and that the people of the firm should follow those decisions no matter what*. The leaders were smart, confident people that felt their decisions were correct. Often, they were correct decisions, in some ways. However, sometimes even the most "correct" decision is not necessarily the best decision. Especially when those decisions affect many people with varying personalities, personal goals, and desires. Lucille Ball said it well: "A man who correctly guesses a woman's age may be smart, but he's certainly not very bright!"

> **"Correct" decisions are**
> **not always the best decisions.**

Leadership did listen to others. But often the opinions of others were discounted, and leadership did not understand or appreciate the need to build consensus among others in the firm. Unfortunately, the leaders that followed Dr. Halff never found themselves worthy "sparring partners," people who could and would have serious discussions with them; people who could expose their weaknesses and help them understand how their blind spots could hold them back from accomplishing some of their personal goals and the goals of the firm. Unfortunately, during that time, the culture was one in which no one felt comfortable pointing out leadership's blind spots.

Leaders who don't have their blind spots exposed to them will not achieve their greatest potential in leading and building a firm.

The leaders that came before me had their blind spots, and I had mine too. I'll expand on that more in chapter 5.

Because of their blind spots, leaders also tend to make poor decisions when it comes to hiring people, because they tend to mirror themselves when evaluating and deciding who to hire. It's called the "halo effect." The reality is that we all do this to a certain extent. We naturally tend to gravitate toward and hire people who are like us. Because, after all, if I am always right, I need people around me who think and act like I do. But nothing could be further from the truth.

We all have blind spots. Our ability to see those blind spots—to become more self-aware of our weaknesses by surrounding ourselves with sparring partners willing to point out our shortcomings—is critical to being a successful leader.

Lacking an awareness of our blind spots will lead to a lack of diverse thought in decision-making and, maybe most importantly, in decisions about who we hire. We need an environment that welcomes diverse thought with open dialogue and debate—yes, debate—to bring out all ideas so the best course of action can ultimately rise to the surface in an open discussion.

> **We all have blind spots.**
> **I have mine. You have yours.**

ONE OF MY BLIND SPOTS REVEALED: I DIDN'T HAVE EMPATHY WHEN I NEEDED IT MOST ...

When I was president, someone worked for me who was a strong leader in our firm and who had been a great contributor. I noticed he was no longer attending meetings or participating in strategic discussions and in fact was showing a victim mentality. He was questioning decisions and not supporting decisions we made or the resulting initiatives, and he seemed to have developed an overall negative view of things. I decided to have lunch with him. During that lunch, he explained that he did not understand the direction of the firm nor did he believe in it. At a deeper level, he felt no one in the firm really appreciated what he did or the value he brought to the firm. He said his clients appreciated his efforts and that he had more connection to them than he did with the people at our company, with whom he had worked for more than twenty years!

His brother had passed away recently. He said he had received numerous emails of condolence from his clients, but nothing from his coworkers or peers. And most riveting, although he didn't say it: nothing from me, his direct supervisor. That was a difficult way to discover my blind spot, but it opened my eyes.

I didn't show him any empathy when he needed it the most. I believe that it is very important for a leader to have empathy, to be able to put yourself into the shoes of the people you are working with. I thought I was an empathetic leader. I was blind to how my actions at times were inconsistent with who I *thought* I was. We all have our blind spots. We need someone or something to help us to open our eyes.

My Turn; Batter Up!

Now, after working with others for years, learning from their successes and failures, it was my time to take the helm of the company. I had watched previous leaders build a stable and reputable firm. I wanted to build upon their success, but I knew there was room for improvement. Just as I also knew there would be room for improvement when it came my time to pass the baton. One important lesson I learned from my predecessors was the importance of high-quality and innovative engineering. It was what set us apart from many of our competitors, and I felt it had to remain one of the cornerstones of our business. At the same time, I knew there was room for more growth opportunity for the firm, more growth opportunity for the individual employee (both career and financial), and more room for employee satisfaction and a collaborative work environment.

Witnessing the previous leaders in action—and observing how people often did not follow their lead but rather worked around them—made me realize ***leadership doesn't come naturally.*** Often, the skills that got you to a leadership level will not help you to succeed as a leader. Nor is being a good leader simply based on a title or position. You must *work* on becoming a good leader, and this means *analyzing what you're doing wrong*. It also means surrounding yourself with people who are different from you. You must create a safe environment in which people can point out your blind spots without fear of repercussions and thus be valuable sparring partners for you.

If you do not, you may create an invisible undercurrent working against you (or around you) that you are not even aware of.

WILL YOU BE A LEADER?

There will be times in your life when you'll encounter a leader who is biased toward people like themselves or someone who doesn't understand how to relate to people. You will have a choice to make: Will you be a victim? Or will you be a leader? Will you become frustrated and disgruntled, or will you work hard to see how you can help that leader—how you can influence that leader? But that is really hard to do. After all, you are telling your boss he is wrong or making a mistake, the very person who has significant control over your destiny. They can fire you; they can raise your compensation—or not. So how do you do this?

45

One technique I learned, very late in my career, is the technique of asking questions. Don't tell the person they are wrong. This immediately puts that person on the defensive; after all, they made the decision after careful thought and believe it is a correct and good decision. Ask pointed questions in a respectful manner about the decision—why they decided what they did. Creating an atmosphere of truly wanting to learn will lead them to a path of exploring the decision and the effects of that decision in a deeper and broader way.

And don't stop with just one question. Ask deeper and deeper questions, with the intent of leading the conversation and the person's thoughts to the point where they will see that maybe the decision needs to be revisited. Maybe they need to change it. It is much more powerful and effective if a person can see the light themselves rather than someone shining it for them. Also, in the discussion you will come to understand their thought process and may in fact see that their decision was not so bad after all, and the best end result may be something in between their approach and yours. That is the ultimate good dialogue that results in the best decisions, outcomes, and direction.

I learned this technique late in my career. I wish I had learned it earlier. Following this approach has allowed me to address very stressful and delicate situations in a very positive and productive way. The outcomes from this approach are far better than avoiding difficult conversations altogether and much better than having conversations that are fraught with emotional stress, overheated from the start because all parties have dug in to their defensive positions.

Try it. It works!

Ultimately, finding a way to have influence—whether it's helping another person see their blind spots or having open dialogue around sensitive, difficult topics—will help you become a better leader yourself.

I THOUGHT ABOUT LEAVING THE FIRM ...

Prior to stepping into a leadership role myself, working under the previous leadership was often frustrating: seeing the inconsistencies in their actions (their blind spots); how it was in conflict with what the culture of the firm had been; seeing how that affected people, including myself—often deflating and de-motivating people, keeping them from doing what was best for the firm; and truly believing that the firm could be so much more successful. I thought about leaving the firm many times. I even interviewed at another firm because I thought I couldn't stand it anymore. Probably the best thing that happened to me is that the other firm didn't offer me a job, so I stayed put. I didn't understand it at the time, but staying and working through those frustrations made me a better leader, and ultimately, I got my chance to lead the company.

You will likely experience something similar. If you are unaware of your blind spots, chances are that some of your people are frustrated and considering leaving *your* firm too.

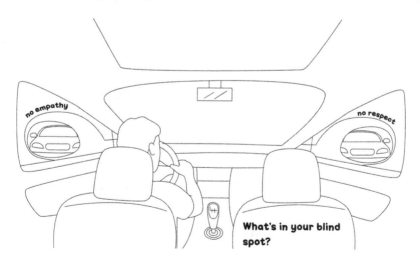

Recognize your strengths and weaknesses and surround yourself with people who complement your weaknesses so you are not blind to them. It is critical to know yourself, know your weaknesses, and be open to criticism. ***Otherwise, your blind spots will undermine your potential for success.*** People will see them long before you do. They will not follow you if you aren't aware of your blind spots and if you refuse to listen to those around you who try to help you see them.

The Epiphany

As I said, working under different leadership after the firm's founder, Dr. Halff, stepped down brought challenging times. Dr. Halff had a true passion for people. He felt that everyone was a contributor and that the company was the place where people should be able to flourish and prosper in their careers. He had created a ***people-first culture***. Leadership that followed believed in that culture but, because their blind spots were never uncovered, were unaware that the firm was drifting from its core values and the culture the founder had created. The decisions that were made were inadvertently inconsistent with that culture. Behind the scenes, people often didn't agree with them or follow them. Oftentimes ***I found myself spending a tremendous amount of time and energy keeping the people within the firm engaged and happy.***

One of the company leaders made periodic visits to various teams and offices. Through feedback I received from these offices and teams, I unfortunately learned that this leader would make statements that people perceived were inconsistent with the firm's culture, sometimes insulting and often deflating the loyalty and drive of the teams and employees. I found myself doing damage control after these visits to reevaluate the topics discussed and the actions taken. Unfortunately, working with this leader to understand the perception and inherent results of his actions wasn't an option because of his leadership style and inability to hear others (his blind spots).

As a result, I needed to assure the offices and teams that, at the end of the day, the company culture and values were indeed still intact. A significant amount of my effort was spent "putting Humpty Dumpty back together again"—building back their self-confidence, their loyalty, and their desire to do great things for themselves and the firm. These meetings and events were very stressful, as I was spending so much time and energy keeping people engaged and preventing employee attrition.

This became a constant struggle and stressor. I was ready to work with the other people of the firm to create growth and opportunity. I felt like the firm and I were held back from what *could* be accomplished. On top of that, when I did try to explain the juxtaposition of my actions with theirs, such efforts were typically not received well. Work just wasn't fun.

SETTLING FOR MEDIOCRITY IS HARD WORK

Dissatisfaction crept into my personal life as well. When I was at home relaxing or when we went on family vacations, I couldn't enjoy being around my wife and kids either. *I knew what the better vision could be but was so frustrated with not being able to fix things*. I wanted to solve the problems that my leaders simply did not see, and I couldn't think of a way to do that. It affected every facet of my life, but I was probably not aware of how deeply it affected me at work and at home. I believe this is true for anyone who cares about the firm they work for—when their *leader's actions and how they interact with people are inconsistent with the culture that is being professed.*

This lack of consistency in leadership becomes a burden on the people who truly care in the organization. It presents a very difficult dilemma when a person loves his or her work but gets stuck in a cycle of constant troubleshooting rather than enjoying forward momentum. Turning off this desire to move forward and instead settling for mediocrity is hard work.

2008—AND BEYOND

For many years I was working at a fast pace with no downtime and a lot of frustration. To make things worse, the great recession hit in 2008. At that time, I was chief operating officer. Working in this environment, in the worst recession since the Great Depression, was an incredible challenge—especially for a person whose goal was to provide career-growth opportunities for people.

Remember the recession of the late 1980s that I spoke of earlier? The one that made previous leaders extremely risk averse? I had not gone unscathed from that memory either. I learned how painful it can be when the downturn comes, and I never forgot that when I took the COO and presidential roles. We made adjustments after the 1980 recession. We built up a safety net financially, with a strong balance sheet and reasonable debt. We positioned ourselves well prior to the 2008 great recession. We did this in the good years by not paying out all the profits and using some to improve the balance sheet—to strengthen the firm. So the balance sheet became something like a savings account for an individual. You pay down debt, you don't

> The great recession hit in 2008. At that time, I was chief operating officer. Working in this environment, in the worst recession since the Great Depression, was an incredible challenge.

borrow quite as much money. You build assets and reduce liability. Then when the downturn comes, you have room for your assets to dwindle or your liabilities to increase. That's what allows companies to sustain throughout the downturn.

Yet even with a strong financial position in a significant downturn, you cannot adjust fast enough to reduce your expenses and maintain profitability—because it's not black and white. No one knows at the start how far down things will go. Just like investing in the stock market, no one really knows, when the drop starts, just how deep the downturn will be. In a professional services firm, 70 to 80 percent of expenses are directly related to employee compensation. The only way to cut expenses sharply is to let people go—but what if the downturn is short? Will you let too many people go? Not to mention the disruption of people's lives—they are not widgets to be adjusted. Inevitably, you cannot cut fast enough, so profits will drop.

Such was the case with the great recession of 2008. I didn't know what the future held, and for the first time ever, *I felt totally out of control and helpless about what I could do to keep the firm stable.* There was no real end in sight for how deep this downturn could be. I remember taking our dogs for a walk with my wife and my daughter and not really being engaged in the conversation. All I could think about was, "How deep will this be? Will the company survive?" I was scared, but in no way could I let anyone know that. And I knew I had to lead while doing *the most distasteful part of my job: letting people go*. Because there just was not enough work in a very tough business climate. I had to stay focused on keeping the company healthy.

One of the biggest reasons why firms in the professional services industry end up selling is because they are not prepared for the downturn. They can't financially withstand it.

Even though the recession of 2008 was longer and deeper than the one in the late 1980s, our improved balance sheet allowed us enough of a nest egg to be able to pay out bonuses. We had also created better metrics to allow for better predictions, more informed decision-making, and the ability to make staffing adjustments quicker.

THE BALANCE SHEET CHALLENGE ...

As a leader you will discover that there's always a fine line between deciding whether you have sufficient cash flow or not. If you're sitting on too much cash, saving too much for the future, then you should be investing. However, if you don't retain enough cash, don't save for the future, will you be able to survive through the next recession or the next unforeseen event? And there will always be a next unforeseen event. The real estate and banking bust of the 1980s, 9/11, the internet bust after 2001, the real estate bust of 2008, and, most recently, the COVID-19 pandemic—what business leader could have ever fully understood and foreseen these events?

Preserving cash, staying stable ...

When times are good, so many employees that walk through the CEO's door have a very good story to tell on why they need that overhead person or why they need to add that overhead expense. To the employee, it seems like the right thing to do. After all, times are good. If the employee doesn't have the battle scars, hasn't yet seen or felt the pain of a deep economic downturn during their business career, they often will not understand when the answer to that new and great idea is going to have to be no.

It's a tough judgment call, but there will be times when your response is, "Yeah, I know you need that overhead person, but we're not going to do it, and here is why ..." It is critical to explain the reasoning for the no. To keep all on board, for them to understand that in the long run—if the firm has a long-term vision of a firm that can sustain itself, to keep as many people as possible during those downturns—sometimes the answer must be no.

Over time, the drip-drip-drip of the constant stress of it all turned me into a curmudgeon, as a good friend, Todd, described me. I didn't realize it was happening. I took offense when he called me that, but now I know he was right. I was on my way to becoming a grumpy old man.

In 2017, the year of my sixtieth birthday, I reached a point of no return. I had two surgeries in the same year, one in April and one in September. Then, in December of that year, I was carrying a bucket of rocks and sand to do some landscape repair in my yard when a sharp, cutting pain ran through my arms, back, and neck. As it turned out, I had damaged nerves in my neck. I was laid up in bed over the Christmas and New Year's holidays.

I took four separate trips to the emergency room as I went through recovery. It was an awful year. I didn't see it coming. It was the most difficult year of my life but, in hindsight, also the best year of my life, because I learned some of the toughest lessons ever. At times I felt hopeless and wondered if I would ever get back to an active, normal life. I became anxious and depressed. I started to see a psychiatrist and a psychologist. I learned that a lot of executives crash and burn after decades of compounded stress. Sometimes you see it; sometimes you don't. I learned that the years of stress in my job, followed by a series of trigger points—multiple traumatic physical medical issues—had triggered deep anxiety and depression. In one session with my psychiatrist, Dr. Madigan said, "Wow, Pat ..." as he exhaled sharply. "It's really sad you haven't had a chance to enjoy the fruits of your labor." I realized that, in fact, I had become a curmudgeon, a grumpy old man. This was my "epiphany"—the turning point in my life.

I was so caught up in fixing the problems at work that I hadn't enjoyed the benefits of success. Nothing about my life—being bedridden, conflicted at work, irritable at home—screamed "success" yet. Before seeing this psychiatrist, I struggled with depression and didn't even know it. I didn't feel secure about my purpose, and I didn't even really know what it was.

Hard to imagine how a successful leader can feel that way, right? But that's how it is with so many in leadership positions.

Today, I will be the first to admit that I suffered from anxiety and depression, but that wasn't always the case. Before all this happened to me, there was no way I would have been open to admitting it and openly discussing it.

You have to be strong as a leader—crisis on the inside, but calm and strong on the outside. And to make things worse—depression? What is that? That is the ultimate in showing weakness. Society has a taboo about depression. The business world doesn't accept it. If you have a physical health issue—a disease of any other organ in the body—society will accept you and offer help in your tough times. But a disease of the brain? The world may be starting to accept and understand this, but the business world sees this internal suffering as a flaw. And to make things worse, men usually refuse to talk to anyone about their emotions. They don't share, until finally, one day, they implode.

Many men (and before all this, myself included) believe that undergoing therapy is a sign of weakness. Now I understand. We are not bulletproof. Everyone understands the science behind a boiling teapot needing an outlet for steam—are our emotions any different? Our emotions play a huge part in who we are, how healthy we are, and how successful we are in our personal and business lives. I made great progress thanks to the therapy I received. Without it, I don't know if I would have ever healed completely—mentally or physically. I now realize how therapy at some level during those stressful times, whether with a coach, a close friend, or a therapist, could have helped me to better handle the challenges and stresses of being a leader. But to do that, to accept that maybe I needed some help and that others could help me in some way, I had to be willing to open up and share my internal thoughts and emotions with others. That didn't happen to me until these major traumatic events occurred. What a much better leader I could have been! And I could have been a much happier person.

> **Find someone to help you.**
> **Don't wait until it's too late.**

These events changed my life. They caused me to reflect and think about my life, my experiences, my career, my relationships with people. This is when I truly realized what my passion in life was (or had been), what my purpose and vision was (or had been), and what it is going forward.

I wanted to work with people, to help them to grow in their careers, to give something back to the people whom I had the privilege to work with and to the organization that had offered me so many opportunities throughout my career.

AN OPPORTUNITY CAME TO GIVE SOMETHING BACK ...

After stepping down as the president, I continued to work at Halff for about a year. During that time, working with the next president, we found a way for me to give back to the company—by mentoring up-and-coming leaders. I started a leadership support group called the Futures Group, which had eleven members. The group format was structured to include a monthly meeting of the group as a whole, as well as monthly one-on-one meetings between each group member and me. The monthly group meetings were structured to have a guest speaker, as well as group discussion time to discuss critical, sensitive issues that would be very difficult to address. Often during the group discussion time, individual members would bring forth challenging business issues, and the group would brainstorm solutions.

The monthly one-on-one meetings created a forum where I could provide direct mentorship and coaching to individual members. At these events, individuals were welcome to bring up any issues for discussion. My approach was not to have the answers for them but rather to ask probing questions to generate discussion and help them to think with great depth and breadth, to analyze for themselves what the best approach to solving a difficult issue would be.

I continued to work with the Futures Group on a contract basis for about a year after retiring. Working with this group helped me have a soft landing after stepping down as president, and moving into retirement—it allowed me to continue to give back after my career had ended. After the formal Futures Group ended, many of the members asked if we could still have lunches and meetings periodically, to which I agreed. This was extremely gratifying for me, because I felt their request was a true reflection of the value that my mentoring had provided—and that I did in fact give something back.

Key Takeaways

- Those leaders who go before us will always have a profound effect on our leadership journey. We can learn from their mistakes and also build upon on their successes. We must engage in self-reflection to be aware of the influences they have on us, both positively and negatively.

- The drip-drip-drip of stressors can erode the well-being of a leader over time. It can happen so gradually that he or she is not even aware of it. These stressors can form a vicious cycle, creating a situation in which the leader doesn't even have a chance to enjoy the fruits of their labor.

Call to Action

1. Are you living a balanced life? How do you know this? What steps can you take to give yourself the time you need to reflect on the business and on yourself?

2. What have you learned from leaders you have worked under? What were the positives? What were the negatives?

3. Are you thinking long term or short term? How does this thinking conform to the company goals? What will you do when it's time to move on from your current leadership position?

4. What can you do to understand the stressors in your life and ameliorate their effect before a crisis forces you to deal with those stressors? Where can you turn for help?

5. When you become the "batter up," what do you want your story to be at the end of your journey?

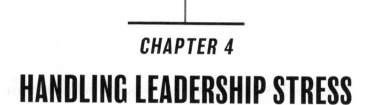

CHAPTER 4

HANDLING LEADERSHIP STRESS

The time to relax is when you don't have time for it.
—SYDNEY J. HARRIS

Every Leader Faces Stress!

Your vision, and your ability to stick to that vision, will be tested every day. One of your primary challenges will be stress, which is inevitable if you are a leader. That stress will cloud your thinking; it will keep you from staying on track and working toward your company's vision and goals. It is vitally important to recognize and deal with that stress before it controls you. If you are a business leader, then ***chances are you have experienced crushing stress at some point in your career***. I'd even bet there's a good chance you're feeling stress now.

However, not all stress is bad for us. We actually need a certain amount of stress to grow and change. But in today's world, it seems that overwhelming stress is the rule and not the exception for many leaders and executives. It's the nagging daily stress that you tell yourself you'll deal with as soon as *this crisis* is over. But that never really happens, because after the crisis is over, you feel good about yourself and think, "Look how great I was, to lead through that crisis. I never missed a beat!"

But what I learned is that while you're living in a pressure cooker with no release valve, you're not capable of acting like your best self. You don't know it, you don't see it—but the people around you do. And most won't tell you because you're the boss! What you don't realize is that you are on the road to burnout. Burnout happens when the pressure is unremitting for too long.

BURNOUT ISN'T GARDEN-VARIETY STRESS

Burnout can manifest itself in many ways. A burned-out executive can feel angry, helpless, trapped, and empty. Physical ailments may include headaches, backaches, insomnia, weight loss or gain, or worse, life-threatening disease exacerbated by stress. Burnout isn't garden-variety stress. *Burnout is unrelenting stress over a period of time* that results in a person reaching a point where something has to give ... and that something will happen sooner or later. But most often, we don't realize it.

I had been leading a company for years when another employee and friend, Terry, saw me in the hall one day and asked me how I was doing. "Great," I said out of habit. He looked at me kind of funny. "You sure you're not stressed? Because I'm worried about you," he continued, looking at me as if he didn't really believe me. I guess he could see it in my face that something was seriously wrong. I shrugged it off and discounted the encounter, telling myself he didn't really know me or what he was talking about. I didn't know what was about to hit me.

> **Many executives are unaware that they're in burnout mode.**

"I am not stressed," I had replied. Then I talked about my fabulous upcoming weekend. Many executives, like me, may not be aware of it when they're in burnout mode. Sometimes they appear cold and detached. Sometimes they self-medicate. Sometimes they become rigid and distant to their loved ones. Sometimes they respond the way I did, out of habit, saying that everything is great, when their physical demeanor says otherwise. Some will just get angry when confronted about it.

Why do I tell you this story? Because it happens to business leaders all the time. And if you want to be a successful leader, you must have a plan in place to deal with it. That plan cannot wait until the big project is finished, because there is always going to be a big project that seems to take precedence. You will tell yourself that. I did all the time!

A Battle Plan for Dealing with Stress

DEVELOP A PLAN FOR TAKING A BREAK BEFORE YOU NEED IT

If stress makes you feel like you are being held captive in your business, you need to think, "What are the things that are keeping me from taking a break?" Then *develop a plan* for taking a break *before* you need it. The notion that, "Oh, I need a break, so I'm going to take two weeks off," is not dealing with stress. That's called a vacation. You are going to feel a lot better, but then you'll go back to the same structure, the same stress. The same people will still be there, and then you'll fall right back into the same rut within a week or two.

A BREAK IS DIFFERENT THAN A VACATION

After a vacation, you may come back feeling recharged for a few weeks, but then you will spiral right back down to where you were before. You have to think about why you need that break so badly and how you are going to find the time and the place where you can think, analyze, and develop ideas and strategies to change the world around you—the world you have created. A break is different than a vacation.

Which one do you need, a break or a vacation? *You* must answer that question for yourself. A break may mean spending time with a close friend, a coach, or a professional counselor. It may be simply spending time with yourself away from everyday distractions. ***For me, a break meant getting away from everything***—work, family, friends. I needed to be by myself for a little "Pat time," to think things through. The break came when I could spend time at my lake house.

My wife and I had purchased the lake house a number of years previously. I didn't know it at the time, but this lake house would become the place for me to unwind, to take that break. It's not like Kathy and I thought about this forever either. We thought about it for about two weeks. We went with a realtor to look at houses and bought the third house we looked at. It actually kind of surprised me that both of us said, "Yeah, let's do this!" It became a retreat for me, and it was my outlet to get away from the stress of things at work.

It was a place where I would sit back, look at the water, and think, "Why am I doing what I'm doing? What do I really need to do? What's most important?" A lot of reflection came from sitting at the lake house by myself, thinking things through. Without the lake house, that kind of deep reflection probably never would have happened, because I wouldn't have had that time by myself, sitting on the deck, looking out over the lake, and having a couple of beers while contemplating life.

I needed the retreat. We all need it, whether we realize it or not. *Where's your retreat?* It can be any place that quiets your mind. When our kids were small, my wife would say that place for her was just the bathtub (no kids allowed, of course!). And now a word of wisdom from that oh-so-great philosopher Winnie the Pooh: "Don't underestimate the value of Doing Nothing, of just going along, listening to all the things you can't hear, and not bothering."

TAKING TIME TO HEAR THE BEAT OF YOUR OWN HEART ...

Doing chores around the lake house and fixing things is something I enjoy. It gives me great satisfaction to accomplish something, even if it's relatively mindless. I enjoy "shutting it down" and not having to deal with the challenges of life. I almost hesitate to say that, because it sounds boring. But maybe a slower pace of life is what we all need once in a while, so we can listen to the beat of our own hearts and reflect on what is most important to us.

You have to find that place or environment that is right for you, where you can take a break and think. Examine the things that cause you stress; *think about what is most important to you*. Imagine how you might change the way you react to the world around you, so the challenges you face can contribute to your growth instead of detracting from it. *These breaks are what helped me deal with, harness, and transform that stress into positive thinking going forward.*

*In today's world, it seems that overwhelming stress
is the rule, not the exception. Take a "break"
to deal with it.*

Living in the Moment

Part of relieving stress is really about getting back to the simple things
in life and enjoying the moment. This is the way we lived as children,
but adults rarely live in the moment. We're always thinking about
what happened in the past or what will happen in the future. Or
we're thinking about what we did wrong or how somebody treated
us poorly or how something went badly.

But what about the present? Leaders are required to be wired for
planning and strategy, but what about the state of contentment in this
one moment? How many times do any of us sit down and think about
what's happening right now? I've discovered the importance of this
very moment and how I don't want to miss it. It's really pretty good!

So how did I learn this? Dr. Goodman, who was the psychologist I saw to pull myself out of the depths of depression after those
traumatic health issues, helped me to see this small but important
part of life. Had that not happened, I probably never would have
learned this lesson.

*The best thinking has been done in solitude.
The worst has been done in turmoil.*
—THOMAS A. EDISON

When I am at the lake house, I love to throw tennis balls to my dogs. That really keeps me in the present. My biggest decision of the day might be, "Should I throw the tennis balls for the dogs right now or throw a little paint on the wall or drive around the lake for a while? Or do I just want to sit, do nothing, and look out over the water and contemplate nature?"

> **Find a way to live in the moment.**

There's something very liberating in immersing yourself in the moment at hand! The here and now. Living in the moment, void of past regrets and future imagined catastrophes, allows one to feel a moment of peace. A moment that feels manageable and nonthreatening during which the stress can dissipate. A moment where you can think about your stress level and what remedial steps you can take to alleviate that stress for the short term. You need a place to escape, relax, and focus your energy on the present. It really doesn't matter where it is. Make sure you have one.

Be Realistic

Five hundred years ago, Michel de Montaigne said, "My life has been filled with terrible misfortune; most of which never happened."

WHAT'S THE WORST THAT CAN HAPPEN?

High levels of stress are often caused by fear of the unknown. The natural tendency of the brain is to gravitate to the worst-case scenario. In the middle of those stressful times, I would back up and ask myself,

"What is causing this stress in me?" And I would always go back to *why* this is causing so much stress and what is the worst-case thing that could happen? Is the worst-case scenario *that bad*? Could I live with that? ***Realize that the worst-case scenario probably won't happen, because you are focused on the issue and working hard on it.***

This helps me to keep things in perspective. It was a big step for me to realize that the chance of the worst-case thing happening was remote and that I could instead turn my stress around by ***focusing on goals that could be accomplished***. You have to decide how you will address these stressful situations and turn them into *positive energy*—working toward whatever is most important to you.

In his article "85% of What You Worry About Never Happens," Charles Black, MD, cites a Cornell University study that "discovered that 85 percent of what people worried about never happened. Of the 15 percent of worries that came to fruition, 79 percent of the time, people handled those problems better than they thought they would."[2]

The Stress of Maintaining Profitability

WHAT DO I HAVE TO DO TO BE PROFITABLE SO I CAN COMPENSATE MY PEOPLE?

Of course, for a business to be successful, it must be profitable. The stress of maintaining or improving profitability is something that most, if not all, business leaders deal with.

Here was my thought process for dealing with the pressure and stress of maintaining profitability: "If I am not profitable, then I

---

2   Charles Black, MD, "85% of What You Worry About Never Happens," published August 17, 2021, https://medium.com/mind-cafe/85-of-what-you-worry-about-never-happens-3f748aab16de.

cannot compensate my employees. If I cannot compensate my employees, they will leave, and then I will have nothing left. But if I can compensate my employees, they are going to stay here for the long haul. If I can do that, then everything else is going to fall into place." So now my thinking turns to, "What do I have to do to be profitable so I can compensate my people?" *This becomes a positive, solution-driven thought process and a plan that is consistent with my purpose:* to drive a people-oriented culture and take care of those employees. That is how I think.

> The stress of maintaining or improving profitability is something that most, if not all, business leaders deal with.

I can't control whether certain things happen or not, but I can position myself to take action so that I can minimize the chance of those bad things happening. I can manage the situation so that the outcome is much better than the worst-case scenario. You know you can't control everything, but at least *you can take steps and actions to keep the worst-case scenario from happening* and instead move things in a positive direction.

The fear of the unknown contributes greatly to our stress. Thinking through the worst-case scenarios begins to alleviate that fear and will result in positive forward thinking. This will help you see what steps you can take to move in a positive direction, *identify growth-oriented ideas and strategies*, and capture *positive visions of what the future will look like*. That thought process helps you articulate to yourself what you're doing and where you are going.

FORGING A PATH THROUGH STRESS

If you can articulate a clear direction in your own mind, you will also be able to express it to other people. ***Stress can become a catalyst that causes you to think things through at a deeper level*** and to set a path forward for others to follow. Now you're leading. You must embrace and believe in the path forward in a visionary manner to be able to tell people what following that path will look like. When you can successfully articulate the path forward, sharing your vision with people, you become more credible. People will believe that you've thought it through, and they can tell that it's not just something you read in a book and said, "Oh, that sounds cool, so we are going to do that." That's not going to feel or sound genuine.

If you embrace that thought process, clearly defining an outcome that will result in something you are truly passionate about, that personal vision will help make you a leader people will follow.

> *Fears and worst-case scenario thinking can become the catalysts for visionary thinking.*

This is the strategy I developed for myself. When I got stressed, fear of the unknown and fear of awful things happening created a lot of the stress in my life. Those fears and worst-case-scenario thinking became the catalysts for visionary thinking, which resulted in stress relief by focusing on positive actions to move forward with.

THE STRESS IS HIGHER WHEN THE STAKES ARE HIGHER

If you're an entrepreneur or an executive in a firm, you work harder than anyone else because you don't want to see the company fail. You know real people have put their hearts and souls into it. Outsiders don't have the same amount of emotional investment as the entrepreneur does. Let me say that again: ***Outsiders don't have the same amount of EMOTIONAL investment.*** The stress is higher when the stakes are higher. However, despite the stress, the path of the entrepreneur or executive can be one of the most rewarding careers out there. For all your hard work, you get to see a business grow, to watch people achieve their goals and grow professionally and personally. You get to be a mentor, teacher, and enricher of lives.

But none of this happens until you use your leadership journey to grab hold of your stress and turn it into an opportunity for growth.

My vision was to create a firm in which people could grow in their careers and work for a long time, maybe even their whole career. It would be a great place to work, where it was all about the well-being and growth of the people. So when I was faced with what seemed like overwhelming challenges—and the stress that goes with those challenges—I would work to harness that stress. I would develop a path forward—a vision, if you will—for how to conquer those challenges in a way that would move us in the direction of my personal overarching vision for the firm and the employees.

The key to bringing a vision to life is to be able to share that vision in a way that people can see themselves as part of and realize how they can personally benefit when that vision is achieved. To do that, you must simplify the vision into one, two, or maybe three clear points that you can articulate clearly, consistently, and repeatedly. People will tend not to be able to see themselves in that vision until they have heard it a number of times and been given time to think about it and digest it. The first time a person hears that vision, they will be critiquing it, trying to understand it, picking it apart—and often trying to find what is wrong with it, why it will never work. After hearing it again and again, they will be able to get past the criticism and begin to understand it and determine a role for themselves within the vision. They will also begin to see how they personally can benefit from being part of the vision—at which point, they now have ownership of the vision. Repetition of the vision is like watching a really good movie over and over—every time you view it, you will see things that you missed the first time you watched it. After watching it several times, the vision of the writer becomes clearer, and you pick up on both subtle and not-so-subtle nuances missed in previous viewings. Suddenly, you have more appreciation for the talent of writers and the quality of the movie than you did the first time you watched it.

My vision was for the firm to grow to over one thousand people while retaining the "culture" of the firm—a culture where people are still most important, a culture where it is almost like a family, as it is in most small firms. A place where the firm becomes a part of who the person is, more than just a career, and a place where a person can spend their whole career and achieve their personal and professional career goals. So my presentation was about growing the firm so we can provide career opportunities for everyone. Everything must advance that goal. That message was repeated in every presentation we did. We would talk about financials—profit and revenue—we would talk about opening offices, we would talk about adding people and more clients. But it always tied back to how it advanced the ability for people to grow in their careers. Whenever an employee presented an idea or a plan of action, one of my first thoughts was always, "How does this tie into our company vision"? I tried to send that message in some way every time I addressed the company in a presentation and in any that I would have. Simple, clear, and consistent. To that end, we created three documents that consistently sent that message:

- Strategic Plan

- Profit Model

- Ownership Model

These will be shared and discussed in greater detail later. These three tools were always about one simple thing: how to advance the ability of people to grow in their careers. The strategic plan of the firm and associated growth goals, achieving profit goals, encouraging employees taking ownership in every task they performed, and the ability to have ownership in corporate stock were all about people's individual growth.

Whatever we did had to support the concept of providing growth opportunities for our people. To accomplish that overarching vision or goal, we knew we had to grow. So there was a constant focus on growth. But why?

> *The overarching goal: growth—to create opportunities*
> *and financial rewards for all.*

Was it all about stock growth? In fact, a significant benefit in growth was to raise stock value, but not only for the purpose of creating personal wealth for the current owners. It was to create opportunities and financial rewards for *all* employees. At our company, common stock was broadly held (over three hundred shareholders), and in fact everyone owned stock through the employee stock ownership plan, or the ESOP, a retirement program where stock distributions were made to all employees based on their compensation level.

It was a light-bulb moment for me during a conversation with one of our young leaders, a person I'd hired years previously. He was describing the good things about our firm and how committed he was to the firm. He also made the point that he saw how I and other leaders before me were able to work for their entire careers at the firm. He saw how our stock value grew and wanted the same experience—to be able to stay at this company and realize the financial rewards that come from increased stock value. Again, *that was the light-bulb moment*!

It all made sense to me. What my mentor Dr. Halff had said and the culture he had tried to create became clear. The young people in the firm wanted the same thing I wanted: *the chance to achieve great things, do meaningful work, and work where leaders cared about them.* They wanted a workplace where they could grow in a meaningful career and reap financial rewards for being committed to their careers and to their company. If this is the culture of the firm—or any firm, for that matter—employees will be inspired, and there will be no limit to the success the firm can achieve.

Understanding this: knowing the overall vision, the reason, the overarching goal helped me keep my eye on the ball and handle the stressful issues of the day. Everything, every decision, revolved around that goal to *inspire, engage, and reward* the next generation of leaders. My vision was not about *me* but about *others* who worked for me.

The message needs to be simple and clear. And once you know what it is, keep your eye on the ball. For me, it was *about people growing*. For that to happen, the company needs to grow. Everything else supported that mission and the passion to make it happen. When stressful times came, there was some relief in being able to deal with that stress by keeping a clear understanding of that mission and ensuring our path forward was aligned with accomplishing it.

The Time for Dealing with Stress Is Now

I TOLD MYSELF I'D SLOW DOWN AT SIXTY

I always told myself I was going to make some personal changes … in the future. I knew I was going to stop working so hard at some point, and I told myself that I'd slow down at sixty. Then, as sixty approached, I said, "OK, I don't want to just step down now. I am going to push it out to sixty-two." Sound familiar? *We often think we can do it later*, especially when we are busy and stressed. Then my wake-up call came: the traumatic events of 2017. The surgeries, the pain that stopped me in my tracks, and the realization that I will not live forever. Something had to change. Now there was no doubt that it *would change*, and I had to stop.

This experience made me realize that you just can't wait until the day comes when you think you want to slow down, retire, or change course to have a plan. You have to make a plan before that day comes; otherwise, you are leaving it to chance—and more often than not, the result won't be anything close to what you envisioned.

What about you? What is your long-term plan? How and when will you stop? Are you going to wait until something hits you so hard you can hardly get back up before you assess and rethink what you're doing—to both yourself and those around you?

Something will happen to you at some point, and you will not be able to continue. Believe it. *You must plan ahead now to cultivate the leaders* who will take the reins from you, maintain the right culture for your business, and create a smooth transition for when that time comes.

WHAT IF YOU DON'T MAKE IT TO YOUR NEXT BIRTHDAY?

There's a chance you will get through the stress of burnout on your own. There's a chance you will live well into your nineties without any health issues. If you are one of those people, that's great. But how can you know for sure? *What if something happens and you can't do next year what you did this past year?* What if you don't make it to your next birthday because you ran yourself into the ground? Do you really want to play Russian roulette with your life—and with the business you worked so hard to build?

Most people who embark on big life changes do it because of a life-changing event that caused them to reflect, take stock of their life, and take action. Don't let that happen to you. Plan ahead. As I ventured through my career journey, I never stopped to take a real break. I wish I had.

It's never too early to think about what happens **after you**. If you think you have stress now, just wait to see what happens if you don't plan for the day when you need to step away and that day comes. If you don't plan ahead for who will replace you, you won't be able to just stop working. Why? Because you are a leader in your business, and there is nobody in place who is ready to take over and do the job successfully. It takes time and training for the next leader to take over. Yes, you can (and may have to) physically walk away from what you have built. However, if you are a leader who had passion for his team and for his business, who put his heart and soul into building something special—something that provides growth and reward for others—it will take a heavy emotional toll on you to walk away from it with no idea of how it will survive the challenges of the future without you. This may take the form of you having to work more years than you wanted to. It may take the form of having to watch your firm decline after you leave, with all the associated negatives—employee job loss, employee opportunity loss, corporate decline, lost revenue and profit. Even clients, who had come to depend on your company, may find themselves upended without one of their most valuable resources.

I have seen several leaders over the years who did not plan for their succession, and an event occurred, sometimes catastrophic in nature, such that they could no longer focus their full attention on their firm. In each case, over time the firm dwindled to far less than what they had created or withered away to nothing. Think about how hard that would be to witness—to see what you worked so hard for all the years of your life, what you put your heart and soul into, diminish or vanish.

So how do you plan for your eventual succession? Just like everything that is important to you, it has to go from something in the back of your mind to something you focus on. Develop a plan, with deadlines, and have someone hold you accountable for meeting those goals and time lines. You must decide: Who will my successor be? Does that person currently exist in the firm? Or do I have to hire someone? How much longer do I expect to be in this position? What level of person is acceptable now, knowing that I can train them up to be able to take my place when the time comes? Once you have identified that person, get another plan ready to identify the following: What are that person's strengths and weaknesses? How do they need to grow? What do they need to learn to successfully fill my shoes? Then begin the process of training and mentoring that person. Just like any goal, you will be successful at the objectives that you are committed and driven to accomplish, and finding your successor needs to be one of them.

If you are successful as a leader, you should always be asking the question, "Who can step up behind me to take my place?"

PLAN AHEAD TO DEVELOP FUTURE LEADERS IN THE COMPANY

Whether or not there is somebody truly ready to take over for you is not the issue here. The point is that you must plan ahead to develop leaders and put them in place for when you are ready to step aside. You can't wait until the day you are ready. It takes time to develop a successor. You have to make a plan and be deliberate about implementing that plan.

Key Takeaways

- You must find a way to handle the stress of leading your team. Your leadership will suffer if you don't take this seriously.

- Be sure you can articulate a clear direction in your own mind that can also be clearly expressed to other employees, repeatedly and consistently.

- Find your successor. Eliminate the stress of not knowing how your team will continue without you.

Call to Action

1. How do you deal with your stress? Do you have a place to go to reflect and think?

2. What is the overarching goal that keeps stress at bay and drives you to excellence?

3. Do you have a succession plan in place?

CHAPTER 5

VALUABLE LEADERSHIP LESSONS

*Everything in life can teach you a lesson. You
just have to be willing to learn.*
—STEVEN P. M. J. WONG

Blind Spots

I talked about blind spots in chapters 2 and 3. This is maybe the most important of lessons learned. I think this concept is so essential to success that I felt compelled to mention it again. The discussion of blind spots has become an essential one for many of the top business journals. Much discussion on this topic can be found in business articles such as *Harvard Business Review*'s November 2020 article "Don't Get Blindsided by Your Blind Spots,"[3] which offers many weapons for attacking blind spots. In this article, the authors note that "most breakdowns in workplace interactions are caused not by bad

---

3   Amy C. Edmondson and Aaron W. Dimmock, "Don't Get Blindsided by Your Blind Spots," *Harvard Business Review*, published November 5, 2020, https://hbr. org/2020/11/dont-get-blindsided-by-your-blind-spots.

intentions but rather by a lack of leaders' awareness of the impact of their behaviors on people in their organization, whether it's a project team, a business unit, or a large corporation."

You can do everything else right as a leader, but if you are not aware of your blind spots, people will not follow you. They will not believe in you, and you will not be an effective leader. All of us have blind spots. We may have the greatest vision in the world with the greatest intentions, *but if we don't recognize our blind spots, we will not see when our actions don't align with our ultimate goals.*

> *Coaches have to watch for what they don't want to see*
> *and listen for what they don't want to hear.*
> —JOHN MADDEN

Get yourself some coaches, people whom you trust who will tell you what you *need* to hear, not just what you *want* to hear. Create an environment where others feel safe coming to you to point out your blind spots. If you operate in an environment where you receive constant positive feedback and very little contrary feedback, you most likely have blind spots that others won't expose out of fear of repercussion.

An example of a blind spot of mine that was exposed to me by others was my instinctive reaction to being confronted. My immediate reaction was to "dig in" and become indignant. Because this reaction was so automatic, it was a very hard habit to break. With time and a lot of deep breathing, I learned to modify this reaction by following up my initial reaction with respectful and meaningful dialogue.

Empathy

LOW ON EMPATHY? SURROUND YOURSELF WITH THOSE WHO HAVE IT

One of the most important lessons I have learned is this: to be successful at creating a people-oriented culture, a culture where people can grow and succeed, a leader must have empathy.

It is critical to put yourself in other people's shoes, to understand how what you do impacts them. If you can't do that, you cannot effectively lead people and articulate to them how the vision and goals that you are passionate about will also help them to achieve their own goals and aspirations. *Ultimately, without empathy on a leader's part, the company will become a sterile corporate environment.* If you don't have empathy, you must surround yourself with people who do. This will help you see your blind spots and better understand how people truly feel about the things happening within your company.

People want to feel heard, listened to, and appreciated!

A lack of empathy can really hurt. It can result in disengaged employees or, even worse, the loss of talented people.

LACK OF EMPATHY LEADS TO A LOST EMPLOYEE ...

At one time, our company had a Chicago office. A young engineer volunteered to go to work in that office. She made it clear that at some point she wanted to return to Texas. After a few years, she decided it was time to come back home, and she did. Shortly thereafter, we had another need for an experienced person in Chicago. She made it very clear she did not want to return to Chicago. However, one of our leaders insisted she was the best person to do the work and "convinced her to go." He told me that she was willing to go back to Chicago. I knew at the time that wasn't true—that somehow he had heard what he wanted to hear or that she told him what he wanted to hear, not what he needed to hear—that she absolutely *did not want to return* to Chicago. She did go back, but six months later she left the firm and moved back to Texas.

Not only did she leave the firm, but she also left the engineering industry. One could argue she was going to change professions anyway, but I don't think so. The leader did not hear or understand where she was coming from. **He was very much a "follow the orders" kind of person. If his leader asked him to do something, he did it.** He could not hear, understand, or relate to the fact that, for her own personal reasons, she desired to establish her life in Texas. She did what she was asked to do, but in the end, she left. Being back in Texas was more important to her than doing whatever it took for her career. He never saw it—he didn't see his blind spot. To him, she simply did not want to be an engineer and would have left anyway. He didn't have the ability to put himself in her shoes, to understand where she was coming from. He didn't have empathy, or he wouldn't have pushed her so far that she quit the profession.

Was I culpable in this? Absolutely. I saw it coming. I had also had conversations with her, and I knew she would not be happy going back to Chicago. But I let it happen. I didn't push back on that leader. I *should* have—at least more than I did! I was not acting as a leader in that moment. The point I am making here is that when things go wrong, most of the time we all have some culpability. When things go south, we cannot just blame it on someone else; we need to look at ourselves and reflect. How did I contribute to the outcome? What can I learn from this experience?

> **When things go wrong, most of the time we all have some culpability.**

People want to feel heard, listened to, and appreciated! People want to come to work and be inspired! But when company leadership lacks empathy, the entire culture is at risk, as people will be deflated and disengaged. Why go to work if you know you're not appreciated? If company leaders can't put themselves in people's shoes and they're making business decisions without thinking at a deeper level of how it's going to affect people, it's going to be a sterile corporate environment.

If you step back and think outside yourself, it's not only going to benefit your people, but it will also benefit your organization. And it'll benefit you to find your own success in helping people grow and flourish.

empathy

You have to find a way to put yourself in other people's shoes if you're going to be an effective leader. You can say you're going to motivate people, but how are you going to motivate them if you have no idea of the pain and challenges your people are going through every day? ***I would argue that you really cannot motivate people. You can only create an environment in which people are inspired***, where they can see that their goals and aspirations can be achieved by working in this place. Then they, in turn, motivate themselves. You have to understand them; you must try to see things from their perspective.

If you're going to have a people-oriented culture and if you want your employees to be motivated and engaged, developing a sense of empathy will be one of the most important things you do as a leader.

Loyalty and Trust

TRUST IS CRUCIAL FOR SURVIVAL IN CHALLENGING TIMES

Lots of books have been written about trust—what it is, how it is created, and how easily it can be lost. I would like to make the point again that having empathy for people—showing that you and other leaders in the organization care about them and understand how decisions affect them—will confirm that you understand their challenges and desires to grow. This is fundamental to creating the building blocks for loyalty and trust that are crucial for survival when challenging times occur. And they will.

In the previous example about the person who we pushed to go to Chicago, I believe it was unfortunate that I had not built enough trust with the employee to come to some type of compromise. Had she truly believed that we had her best interest, as well as the company's best interest, at heart, we could have retained this employee. When I reflect back on this situation, I can totally understand how the necessary bonds of trust had never been established with this employee, which would have paved the way to have open, meaningful dialogue.

Later in my career, we had an exemplary employee who needed to relocate, because of his wife's educational pursuits, to a city where we didn't have an office. Though more difficult and less efficient for the company, we worked with him to accommodate this requirement by allowing him to work long distance at a time when that practice was not common. He later returned to our main office and became a true leader. However, at one point he became overwhelmed with responsibilities and was working exorbitant hours. When other firms recruited him, instead of just leaving, he gave us an opportunity to make adjustments to his situation to retain him. If it had not been for the bonds of trust we had built with him years earlier, he would not have stayed on with our company. Our earlier actions had demonstrated to him that we cared about him personally and not just what was best for the company. This story shows that empathy, loyalty, and trust are interconnected. If a leader demonstrates empathy, loyalty and trust will ensue.

> If it had not been for the bonds of trust we had built with him years earlier, he would not have stayed on with our company.

Another example of this was a time when one of our employees' family members became very ill—with a difficult illness. The family member needed extended healthcare in another city. The employee requested to work remotely during this period. This was long before the technology existed to allow working remotely in an effective *or* efficient way. We knew that there would be a cost for this and that the person could not be truly effective working in those conditions. However, we also knew that as an overall cost to the company, it would be insignificant to the overall financial performance and profitability of the firm.

Had we been operating strictly by the numbers, we would have said no. That person would have either left voluntarily or we would have let them go, and we would have simply hired another person. The employee worked remotely until they could return home. What was the result? That employee stayed with us and became an effective leader in the firm—with loyalty to the firm that will never go away. Through this situation, others in the firm also saw that we were true to our values—we really did care about people and would help them when possible. It was not just about the numbers.

These are the things that people will remember when another firm calls and offers them a job or when they get frustrated for one reason or another. They will remember that this firm is more than just about business. They will be loyal and work hard to get past challenges and frustrations rather than simply giving up and going to work for another firm. This is the kind of loyalty and trust that will keep good people for a long time—maybe for their entire career.

People become engaged and motivated when

1. they feel valued, respected, and connected with the leaders of the firm;

2. the values of the firm and the firm's leaders are consistent with their own values; and

3. they feel that they are contributing to the vision and goals of the firm.

Adherence to the overall vision and values of the firm during good times as well as challenging times is essential for the company to build employee loyalty and trust and sustain itself over the long haul.

A CULTURE OF EMPATHY MEETS THE CURVEBALLS

When the curveballs come (and they will), you may feel like every-thing and everyone is against you and the company. But if you have set the stage prior to the tough times by defining and articulating the vision and core values of the company and by engaging your employees and showing them empathy—and *then holding to those core values during those more difficult times*—you and the company will survive and thrive. Loyalty and trust will shine through.

YOU CAN'T FORGET ABOUT THE PEOPLE ...

Leaders are under a lot of pressure. No one is immune to it. You have to make incredibly difficult decisions, and there are times when it feels like everyone is against you. If your goal is to have a sustainable company over time, you're always thinking about what's next. That means you need to factor in revenue, profit, and economic projec-tions—but no matter what happens, you can't forget about the people. Engaged people make it all happen.

> *People become engaged and a deep level of trust and loyalty evolves when leaders have empathy and truly understand and care about the challenges their employees face.*

Getting the Right People

KILLING THE OFFICE DRAMA—*PEYTON PLACE* NO MORE!

When I joined the management team as chief operating officer in 1997, I immediately became aware that some people were only looking out for themselves. These people were deceitful and concerned mostly with making it to the top, not the overall success of the organization.

It didn't happen overnight, but we cleaned it up over time. Some people left the company on their own, others were let go, and some changed the way they behaved and how they treated others. We hired a lot of new people. Some of them fit, some of them didn't, but over time we eliminated drama within our offices. We *developed a culture of respect* for and among everyone at the firm. The people who didn't fit the culture had to go. Even though those were tough decisions, great leaders make it work for the rest of the team. If the leader fails to make these tough decisions, that leader is not respecting those within the company that truly adhere to the company's vision. How can the leader expect others to follow his or her vision if the leader refuses to enforce that vision?

I expect people who are in it for themselves and cause drama within a firm exist in all companies. A leader has to be willing to address these issues for the firm to truly reach its goals.

A CULTURE OF RESPECT WHERE EVERYONE REAPS THE REWARDS ...

I somehow knew that if we could create a culture of respect, a culture of teamwork, where people would work together for a common good, the firm would flourish. Everyone would reap the rewards—much greater rewards than if people worked primarily for themselves. A secondary focus was to create a culture of *ownership*. We wanted people to take ownership in what they were doing and have a sense of pride in their work, no matter how large or small the task.

People who didn't fit this "people first; own it" culture were either let go or decided of their own accord to leave after some candid conversations about the culture of the firm and what behaviors were required for them to be successful in the organization.

MANAGING THE CONSULTANTS

Most management consultants say you have to have people in the right seat on the bus, and that some people who don't fit need to be let go. *The consultants will tell you to get rid of the dead wood, bad apples, or people who don't fit your culture.* They will advise you to do personality profiles to help figure all this stuff out. And if people are not a fit, get rid of them. *For me, it's not that simple.*

A personality profile helps, but it can't show action and execution. A personality profile doesn't tell you what anyone is like in day-to-day business, in the heat of the most stressful times. Nor will the personality profile tell you who will be willing to open their mind to changing and embracing a culture in which they can succeed. Further, the person is often bringing great value in some areas but not others; maybe he or she can succeed with the right tools and support. It's a balance between the value the person brings versus the disruption that comes from that person—and whether the person can grow and change. If it were as simple as picking and choosing your people by personality profiles, anyone could do it, and everyone would do it.

RIGHT PERSON, WRONG SEAT ...

Here is an example of how it's a balancing act and therefore difficult to make these decisions. One of our employees proved himself a capable employee in a well-established, successful, and stable office within the firm. He later moved to lead a new office in a growing area. His skill set was not a good fit for being an office leader. Leading an office and operations was not his gig.

He simply didn't have the heart to tell people what they needed to hear. He didn't tell them the whole story; he tried too hard to make them all feel good, which gave the impression he was not being honest with them. He was a loyal, twenty-year-plus employee. Did he have the success of the firm at heart? Absolutely he did. I could have said, "We need to let him go because he doesn't fit any of the established positions at our firm." But I didn't because of the impact it would have had to the culture of our firm and what it would show about the kind of firm we were. He had a lot of experience and a long tenure and was incredibly loyal to the firm.

I had to believe there was a place where he could make a difference and bring value to the firm. There was a challenge in trying to move him to a new position because there was really only one path to leadership—to lead an office. This required overseeing a substantial number of employees in an operations role—not his strength. However, one thing he was really good at was creative marketing—developing and creating projects that benefited our clients. So we found a way to make it work. We created a position using those skills. We essentially had to think outside the box to create a new box. We created a new position for him where his main responsibilities would include developing creative marketing strategies to brainstorm and develop new ideas and projects that would solve our clients' problems. Thus our work and revenue from existing clients would increase, and we'd expand our client base with new and innovative solutions. Managing a lot of people would no longer be part of his job description. Other challenges to moving this employee to a new position included trying to find a way to help him feel comfortable—assuring him this was an important and meaningful role. He needed to understand that he was still an important person in the firm, that he was still growing in leadership, and that he was still a key person who was vital to the organization. It was also important to communicate the importance of this new position to the rest of the company, so all could understand how leadership was working to invest in creating opportunities for valuable employees—not demoting them.

Our communication efforts must have worked, because he took the position and **became incredibly successful!** He worked with clients and thought, "How do I solve their most difficult issues and problems?" He was doing what he was passionate about and what he was great at. So it wasn't about getting him out of the company; we needed to place him in the *right seat on the bus*. The result: rather than pushing him out, we gave him the opportunity to grow and excel in his career, **and we developed a great employee and leader who brought in lots of revenue**, took great care of clients, and taught the next generation how to do it.

This story also serves to point out how important coaches can be. I will expand on this later, but in this example, moving that office leader to a position where he could be successful—creating projects, building a practice—may not have happened without the help of a coach who drove me to think deep and hard to find the right solution.

When it comes to deciding whether a person is the right fit or not, you must understand deep down what that person is all about. Does that person fit the culture and values of the firm or not? Are they open to change? A personality profile can help, but it cannot by itself answer these questions.

It's easy to think someone is not the right fit when they are not fitting in, but it may simply be because they don't have the right tools for success or they're not in the right seat on the bus. Because of this, they may be incredibly stressed and very unhappy. They may be spending tons of time and energy on trivial things that really don't matter to them, thus disrupting their world, both work and personal, with their lack of focus.

ARE THEY IN THE RIGHT SEAT? ARE WE GIVING THEM THE TOOLS TO SUCCEED?

Don't give up too soon on a person who has the potential to be a great contributor and future leader. I can't emphasize this enough: *Leaders are not born; they are created.* You have to commit to working on leadership traits and help people see their strengths and weaknesses, putting them in places where they can succeed and prove their value to the company. People's worst qualities are revealed when placed under the stress of being in the wrong position. It may be easy to draw the conclusion that they are disruptive and need to be let go. On the other hand, sometimes stress is a good test to show what a person's character is truly made of and can help you make the decision you need to make as a leader. What is the right seat on the bus for them, and can they ultimately fit into the culture of the organization?

NOW WE HAVE A HOLE TO FILL

What you must remember is that every time you let someone go, you also create a void that must be filled. There is no magic formula for finding the right person to fill that void—or, stated another way, *there is no guarantee that the next hire will be a good hire!*

When you're looking for a person to hire—to fill a void after someone left the organization, voluntarily or involuntarily—it will be very difficult to find the person who fits exactly. Every individual is different, and you may find a really good candidate who checks some of the boxes, but not all—yet has some other great qualities.

THE FIVE-TOOL LEADER ...

The ultimate leader is a five-tool leader. What is a five-tool leader? It is like a five-tool baseball player. A five-tool baseball player has speed and a strong throwing arm, is a good fielder, has a high batting average, and has the ability to hit for power (extra bases).

Very few baseball players excel at all five—and throughout baseball history, very few players are considered five-tool players. There's a few you may recognize: Willie Mays, Mickey Mantle, Hank Aaron, and recently, Billy Beane, who was made famous with the book and movie *Money Ball*.

From my experience in the professional services industry, I developed my own list of the skills that the ultimate leader, the five-tool business leader, would have. I believe that these tools apply to any business, but they may vary to some degree.

1. Great ability to inspire and lead people/employees: able to train and mentor others with a clear vision of what they and the company are trying to achieve, so people respect and follow them
2. Great communication skills: good at communicating and developing a trusted relationship with clients—the ability to become a trusted advisor to their clients
3. Great sales skills: able to win new clients and new business

4. Great technical skills: has competence in their field of practice and a thorough understanding of the workflow process so they can manage and lead the operations and direction of the team or company

5. Great financial knowledge: has a solid understanding of the financials that underpin the business and thus the ability to drive profitability for the team or company

Just as the five-tool baseball player is a rare gem, so, too, is the five-tool leader. Very few leaders truly excel in all five areas. To be successful, the leader must understand their strengths and capitalize on them, and, more importantly, recognize their weaknesses—accept them—and surround themselves with people that will provide the tools they are missing.

Are you a five-tool leader? If not, what tools are you missing? Who can bring the tools you are missing to the table?

Are you trying to fill a position by looking for the five-tool player? If so, you are reducing your chances for success, because your expectations are too high. Evaluate the tools that the applicant brings to the table and determine if they can succeed with those skills, complemented by others in the organization.

Are you expecting your current leaders to be five-tool players? Are your expectations too high? Maybe you need to recognize their strengths, put them in a seat on the bus where they can succeed and support them with others who will help them in their weaker areas.

Do you have a potential five-tool leader in your organization? Have you recognized them? Have you given them the opportunity to grow and excel—so that they don't become frustrated and leave, taking their talents to another company?

I SIMPLY COULD NOT FIND THE RIGHT PEOPLE

At one point, I was frustrated that I simply could not find the right people and could not get people hired. I finally realized that I was being too rigid. *The lesson I learned was that I needed to be more flexible and creative.* A good sports metaphor for this is when a coach can't find the exact recruit he needs, he chooses the best athlete instead! In business, hire the best candidate, even if he or she doesn't fit the exact qualifications. Be creative about how that person can fit into the organization, and let the organization morph a bit as it brings that person in and allows them to excel with their skills. No one fits exactly. *The best fit will be when the new hire changes to fit the organization and the organization changes a bit to fit their skills.*

Often some of our new hires came from companies with very different structures, including firms that were much larger. It was a great opportunity for us to have new people bringing new ideas, innovations, and new ways of thinking. However, on a cautionary note, new hires also brought the opportunity to erode the core values of the organization. As the leader, my job was to be vigilant about this while still looking for opportunities to access the positive new ideas that hires brought.

A NEW HIRE LEADS TO CHANGE ...

In the case of one critical new hire, we realigned an entire business line based on ideas he brought, which made our operation better. We came to understand that this particular business line had too many long-term employees that were stuck in doing things their own way, because that's the way they had always done it. While some were resistant to the change, because we improved the performance of the business line and maintained our core values at the same time, we eventually gained acceptance.

Leaders have to look at the big picture! Retention, training, and letting people go are costly, but so is *keeping* people who aren't the right fit. Building a firm means hiring and retaining people who can contribute and who fit the culture and direction of the firm. Do they fit? How much is it going to damage the bottom line if they don't work out? Look at the revenue they are bringing in; what will be lost? On the other hand, how is it going to affect our culture if they stay? Are they not fitting in because they are not in the right seat? Maybe they *can* succeed if we put them in the right position. It's a balance. It takes time to do it right and be successful.

You are going to watch people leave—or worse yet, you will let people go and wonder why they are doing so well *over there*. *A lot of it is about looking at the person and asking, "Are they in the right seat?"* Do they have the right skills to succeed? Am I giving them the tools they need to succeed? Am I giving them the opportunity to succeed?

LEAVING THE FIRM TO SUCCEED SOMEWHERE ELSE ...

We had a young project manager who was one of our rising stars. He was heavily recruited by another firm, because he was so talented and people in the industry knew it. He received offers several times from that firm. His stated reason for wanting to leave was because of the money—the more lucrative offers he was being given. In reality, the offers *were not more*; they were presented in a creative way to make it *look* like he would receive more compensation. Twice, we had good, open conversations, and we were able to show him that.

The third time he came with an offer from that firm, I simply said to him, "It's not about the money; we proved it to you twice. You need to decide where you want to work." He decided and left. He went to work for the competitor and was incredibly successful. Admittedly, he grew in his career much faster than if he had stayed with us. **So why was he so successful at that firm, and not at our firm?** Because he was in the wrong seat at our firm. He was being held back in the seat he was in. He had grown into much more of a leader than we could see. We held him down as a project manager, when in reality his talents were much broader than that. He had great potential as a leader growing a business line within the firm, rather than being a project manager in a highly technical role. I didn't see it; I missed it. When put in the right seat—that of a leader in more of a manager-leadership role rather than a technical project manager role—he flourished.

Do you have everyone in their optimal seat?

Look carefully at the seats people are in. Are they in the right seats, and are they being given the tools and opportunities to succeed?

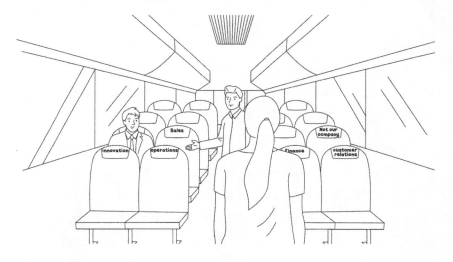

Looking back over my leadership journey, I realize that a significant amount of my efforts and the management team's efforts were involved with actually putting the right people in the right places. If an employee wasn't succeeding in one area, we were always looking at where we could put them so that they could be successful. If we had a need, instead of just looking at external candidates and saying, "Let's go hire somebody to fill that role," we would typically look internally first. Was there someone who could *grow* in their career by being moved into that position? It was truly a strategic chess game, one involving knowing the skills of each employee and then moving them to the most effective place on the board.

Often, we would search internally by advertising a position within the company. Sometimes we approached an individual. When we advertised a position internally, we never advertised salary, because we wanted people who were motivated primarily by a growth opportunity and not just by financial considerations. We wanted people who trusted the process and knew if they embraced the culture of growth, opportunity and quality performance that appropriate compensation would follow. Employees, for the most part, knew that if you were driven—committed to growing personally and to growing the company—then other things, like compensation, would fall into place. Those who had spent a number of years with the company learned this by watching the career trajectory of those who "bought into the system." They could see the long-term careers that were being established and the personal and financial fulfillment inherent in those careers. They could witness the attitudes of successful long-termers who had a more global company vision.

THE GLOBAL VISION ...

I'd like to expand a little more on what having a global vision entailed. Our company was a multidisciplined firm, meaning we did architecture, civil engineering, mechanical engineering, landscape architecture and planning; the list goes on. Some practices, at times, were more profitable than other sectors were.

However, we recognized that even if you were in a lesser-profit sector, you should not get financially dinged for that, because it was often just inherent in the nature of that sector. Our focus had to be on the fact that it required all those disciplines working together to make the company successful. For instance, we had a landscape architecture and planning group that did a lot of land planning and municipal planning. That group was one of the lower profit margin entities. There just wasn't as much money in that industry as there was, say, in the transportation field.

But the work they did was very visible, much more graphic and creative in nature. It made our company look like more than just a stuffy engineering firm. The landscape architect group, with their graphic capabilities and the creativity they brought to projects, helped clients to see us as a firm with a more holistic view. Engineers are often stereotyped as those people with pocket protectors who don't under-stand society and don't really care as long as their results are functional. After all, if a concrete drainage channel will work, why use a grass-lined channel? The concrete channel is more functional and uses less land. Add the landscapers and land planners to the mix, and now we have a different dynamic, a company that really thinks more holistically about the impact it has on society as a whole. Perhaps a grass channel / green belt area is worth the extra land, and maybe aesthetic veneers on bridge columns are worth the cost.

So the planning group's profits weren't that high, yet they played a much bigger role in the overall *value* of the company. They set us apart from competitors when we would go after projects, because our clients saw that we were going to bring a solution that was more than just a road from here to there. It would be a road with amenities and beautiful trees, one that would engage the community. With the engineers and the planners working together, it was the perfect blend of sound engineering and aesthetic investment in the community. Top notch employees were willing to work in the less profitable sectors because they knew their value would be understood and rewarded. They bought into the idea that financials were about the company as a whole, not individuals or individual profit centers.

Part of the company's global view also meant knowing that creativity and innovation would be rewarded. A fertile environment was created when employees felt safe speaking out. That led to more employees being willing to take more calculated risks, because they knew even if something they tried didn't work out as planned, they weren't just going to get beat over the head or financially dinged.

The company's global view also meant having a true understanding of the cyclical nature of different sectors. The sector that is on top this year won't stay there. All groups will have their ups and downs. One can look at the recent COVID-19 pandemic to see how a totally unexpected event could invert industries. Brick and mortar stores out; Amazon warehouses in. With the advent of the new work-from-home opportunities, suddenly congestion and the demand for new roads didn't seem to be of such paramount importance. Having an understanding of the cyclical nature of business sectors gave the company leadership the ability to focus on the importance of the financial solvency of the business as a whole, rather than focusing on individual profit generating centers. Those that embraced this idea saw the pros of this system outweighing the cons in the long run.

Going back to finding the right people: often, when we advertised internally for career opportunities, we got little to no response. And we found that candidates who were a good fit for a growth opportunity were reluctant to make the move. I attribute this to human nature—because in general, most people tend to be risk averse. People are often comfortable in a position where they have had success. There is a fear of moving into the unknown, taking on new challenges, learning new skills, an inherent aversion to risk—they knew they might fail at a new endeavor.

Fortunately, we also found that this employee hesitancy toward new challenges could be overcome by assuring the candidate that they would have full support and would be given the needed tools, training, and time to succeed. When this is clearly articulated along with the potential benefits for growth in their career, the aversion to risk could be overcome. The rewards would begin to outweigh the risks. These are some of the reasons why it is so critical for leadership and management to build trust.

You've got to have people who trust the leadership, who want to be a part of the team, and who believe that being a part of the team and where it is going is truly in their best interest. Without this belief instilled in your employees, you will have little chance of employees taking on that risk and moving into their correct position—that of a winning position for the employee and the company.

Conversely, there will be times when a leader needs to dissuade an employee who expresses interest in a position that is not a good fit for them. In this situation it is imperative to outline, without demoralizing them,

> People are often comfortable in a position where they have had success. There is a fear of moving into the unknown, taking on new challenges, learning new skills, an inherent aversion to risk—they knew they might fail at a new endeavor.

why the position is not a good fit for them. If the leadership team has a track record of finding good fits for its employees, it will be much easier for employees to accept this outcome.

When the Going Gets Tough

How can you really have empathy when you're letting people go?

Leaders have to do things they don't want to do in the name of the business, and sometimes it ruins friendships and disrupts lives. You have to do the best you can and trust that it's all for a purpose and the betterment of the company. A leader is evaluated on results, not emotion, and often the board of directors or whoever a leader reports to isn't really concerned with much else. Results matter. And unfortunately, that includes letting people go.

The most difficult time I ever experienced as a leader was the economic downturn of 2008, when we had to let people go. As I am someone who cares deeply about employees and their welfare, I found it a very stressful time. But the truth is that a leader can't expose that personal side when it's time to make tough decisions. *I told myself that when the day comes that we let people go and I don't care about it, that's the day I need to step down from being a leader.* For me, there is nothing worse or more difficult than letting people go because you don't have work for them. But that's the job of the leader—to make the tough decisions, no matter how distasteful they are.

WEEPING ON THE BALCONY ...

During the 2008 downturn, it became apparent that a "reduction in force," a layoff, was necessary. One of the people on that list was a good friend of mine, a person I played golf with, a person who hosted my thirtieth-birth-day surprise party. Nevertheless, it had to be done. I, as the leader, could have delegated that to someone else, but I felt it was right for me to do it since he was a friend.

On a day I will never forget, I flew to Houston—forgot my luggage, by the way—and met with my friend. I told him the time had come for us to part ways, due to a lack of work. It was one of the most difficult things I have ever done. My oldest daughter lived in Houston at the time, so I stayed over with her that night. Late that afternoon, I got to her apartment before she got home, sat on her balcony, and wept.

Hard decisions like layoffs that personally and adversely affect others—that's the side of leadership that none of the leadership books talk about, the side that no one fully understands, until they're sitting in the chair. That's when you realize that it's often very lonely at the top. Difficult things have to be done, but carrying them out with *respect* is what makes a great leader. Empathy at that moment means doing what has to be done is the most respectful manner possible and understanding you are doing what has to be done is in the best interest of the company and the people of the company as a whole. People will see you making those tough decisions and will ultimately trust that you, as the leader, have the company and the employees' interests at heart. But it will take time for that trust and understanding to develop.

During those dark days of the 2008 downturn, people started to lose confidence that we were the people-oriented firm we said we were. Some thought we had become heartless. I still have a little statue on my desk of the Tin Man from *The Wizard of Oz*. It was given to me by a good friend, Joni, the head of our human resources department. She saw how people had lost trust that the leaders of the firm and I believed in and cared about our employees, and she observed the stress I was under. She gave it to me and said, "This is a reminder that despite what people may say, you really do have a heart; you really do care about the people." We were facing the greatest recession since the Great Depression, but people still didn't fully understand or accept the necessity for layoffs. Employees were viewing the situation with emotion instead of logic. I didn't have that luxury. It was uncharted waters, and I had to make the tough choices, whether people understood or not. We lost a larger percentage of our workforce than we had ever lost before. Knowing that we were faring better than most of our competitors under the harsh economic conditions didn't ease the heartache. It was brutal. We tried to help laid-off employees find other work, but there was only so much we could do when the economic conditions were so dire.

Because of the layoffs, the trust that people had in me and in the leadership of the firm eroded during that time. The good news is that we were able to rebuild that trust during the years that followed, because we stayed true to our core values—that it's all about people and respecting people, no matter what. Yes—laying people off sounds contradictory to respecting people. But laying people off had to be done for the health of the firm as a whole. In retrospect, I believe people eventually saw that we only did what we had to do to survive and that, ultimately, by making those difficult decisions, we were able to maintain the jobs for most of the people within the firm.

You will survive if you don't lose sight of your overall vision and values.

No one enters leadership understanding everything that's involved. There will be times when *you have to let people go*. It's part of the job, because if you didn't, you'd be irresponsible by keeping underperformers or mismanaging the business. Other times, you will lose friends or employees to a competitor, feel betrayed, or get feedback that's inconsistent with how you see yourself. You must stick to your core values—and your overarching vision—during those times. When people leave the firm, voluntarily or involuntarily, treat them with respect—always. When someone leaves voluntarily, learn from the experience. Ask yourself how you contributed to their decision to leave.

STAYING THE COURSE DURING A DIFFICULT TIME ...

I once had an employee that I had hired right out of college. He worked for me for many years. I trained him, mentored him—and he became my right-hand man, so to speak. He received an offer from another firm and decided to go to work for that competitor. I, of course, became angry and frustrated that after all I had done for him—trained him, taught him everything he knew, molded him into a very good engineer—he was going to betray me, to leave and go to work for another firm.

Fortunately I went home first and calmed down before I approached him. When I talked to him the next day I still tried to keep him—but in the end, he decided to leave. I respected his decision that he believed this new position at another firm was the best opportunity for him and wished him well. We parted ways with mutual respect. What I realized later is that I was so fortunate to calm down before I met with him, rather than what I wanted to do the day he told me he was leaving—berate him and tell him what a bad decision he had made.

Why was it fortunate to have calmed down? Because he had friends and peers who worked at our firm. They saw that I was disappointed that he was leaving, of course, but that I still treated him with respect. I was true to my values, and thus they gained trust in who I said I was and that my values would prevail even during the most difficult and frustrating times. Had I acted with frustration and anger,

> the opposite would have prevailed, and I would have lost the confidence and trust of the people who worked for me while at the same time undermining the very core values that I had worked so hard to drive home.

How you and the company react during the most difficult times will truly define your firm's culture. During the downturn after the 2008 recession, we unfortunately had to let people go, and there were layoffs. The easiest thing would have been to look at individual offices and simply cut staff in places where the teams and offices had no work. However, our long-term goal prior to the recession was to open offices in new locations with the understanding that this approach would result in growth for the firm and career-growth opportunities for the individual. Based solely on workload during the recession, we would have closed some of our offices that we had recently opened—offices that had not been there long enough to become established with sustained workload. But we had committed to offices in these locations, and it was critical to our long-term growth—and in turn the ability to provide opportunities for people in the long term.

So we did not simply close the offices when they had no work. We worked with the leaders to share work across the company, to keep the recently opened offices—and to keep the best people, no matter where they were located. This solidified the culture: "We are all in this together. It's about teamwork; it's about working together for the firm as a whole. An individual office or team may have to share work today—but someday that favor will be returned. The firm will do much better in the long term if we have a culture that promotes working together to facilitate growth for the firm and, in turn, growth for the individual in their career."

During the great recession of 2008, we also stayed true to our fundamental value of providing high-quality work. As mentioned previously, quality and innovative work is often what differentiated us from our competition. At a time in which supply versus demand for engineering services necessitated cutting fees to clients to stay competitive, we could have cut back on the quality of services provided to reduce our costs. However, it was not an option for us, as this was one of our core values. Bad times were no exception. Our passion for quality services was not only enforced during good times but during the downtimes and in the most difficult situations as well.

If you as leader hold true to your long-term vision and values, you will build long-term loyalty and trust in employees, and this will solidify that culture.

Even though it may not have appeared that way, I was pained by the loss of every person we had to lay off during the downturn. As difficult as that period was, it would have been even *more* painful and hurt even *more* people if the company did not survive.

Key Takeaways

- Blind spots: get yourself some coaches, people who will tell you what you need to hear—not just what you want to hear.

- Hire the best candidate, even if they don't fit the exact qualifications. Holding out for the perfect candidate can leave you frustrated and empty handed.

- Be creative and flexible in your company's structure to open up new or better-fitting positions for your employees.

- Don't let hard times erode your company's culture. Trust and long-term loyalty will depend on it.

- You must have empathy. That includes having empathy for everyone in your company and balancing empathy for the individual with the need to safeguard the financial solvency and stability of the company. Sometimes this will include layoffs or termination of an employee who is undermining the culture. Always be respectful!

Call to Action

1. Evaluate your empathy by finding trusted confidants who can give you honest feedback. Make sure your circle of confidants includes those that will offer you counteropinions and food for thought. They should be people who complement (not compliment!) your skill set. Ask lots of questions that will ensure honest feedback. If you are not being challenged enough to get your feathers ruffled from time to time, you are probably not surrounding yourself with those who feel comfortable challenging you.

2. In the end, you will be the only one who can determine whether your leadership expresses an adequate amount of empathy or whether adjustments need to be made—but this self-reflection cannot be done in a vacuum.

3. When something goes wrong, ask yourself what your culpability is in the situation.

1

CHAPTER 6

COACHES AND PARTNERS

Everyone needs a coach. It doesn't matter whether you're a basketball player, a tennis player, a gymnast or a bridge player.
—BILL GATES

Reflection—Great Leaders Don't Lead Alone

Great leaders don't lead alone. They have a support team. There will be some very difficult times. A strong leader understands this and finds a way to persevere and work through those difficult times.

My wife of thirty-seven years, Kathy, has been an instrumental part of my support team. She is also a professional engineer and has worked in the industry for many years. Kathy understands what the consulting engineering world is like and the stresses that go along with it.

Kathy stayed at home while we were raising our children. Those were great times, but I believe they were also the most stressful, most difficult times in our marriage. To quote Charles Dickens, "It was the best of times, it was the worst of times."

I was grateful she was there, taking care of our children at home. But being the stay-at-home mom, the PTA mom, wasn't totally fulfilling for her. She did get great satisfaction out of being there for our kids as they were growing up, but she really missed being challenged from a professional and intellectual perspective. I didn't help much that when I came home, I was wiped out.

My kids still say jokingly today that once it got to be about eight o'clock, you didn't talk to Dad, because nothing he said made sense anyway. My wife wanted to get out of the house and do things, because she never got out. I just wanted to relax at home. *Achieving work-life balance was challenging.*

There were times when we both felt somewhat underappreciated. How could she know what it was like to have to deal with people and business issues all day long? How could I possibly know what it was like not to get to interact with adults all day long? I got to be away all day, growing in my career, learning and achieving; she got to witness all the special moments of our children's lives, forging a much stronger relationship with our kids. It was a difficult season to navigate together. The realization that nobody gets to have it all hit us like a sledgehammer at some point.

IT WAS ALL ABOUT THE KIDS. IT WAS ALL ABOUT WORK. SOUND FAMILIAR?

Those were some difficult times, arguing with each other over little things—I am convinced much of it was stress induced—but we were committed to the marriage, our kids, and making it work. Neither of us really totally understood the other's world, but we muddled through. Every weekend was filled with sporting events or other kid activities. It seemed as though we never got to do anything we really wanted to do, because it was all about the kids. It was all about work. Sound familiar?

A lot of married couples are on that roller coaster; they see no end in sight and just want to get off. All too often it ends in divorce. ***Recognize that these stressful times are seasons of life, and they will not last forever.*** In the end, there will be incredibly rewarding memories from these periods of life—all the more reason to understand what is most important to you so you can focus your energy on the positives.

During the most stressful times, it is so important to keep the ones that are closest to you *close to you* and not just give up. During those stressful times—even though they were difficult for my wife and me—we supported each other. That support is necessary to make it through the hardest of times. The people closest to you must be your confidants—and vice versa. It's easy for them to give up on you and for you to give up on them. Try your best not to; instead, work through it together. You need that support, and so do they! Keep in mind that the role your loved ones play is a key role, but they are not meant to be your sole source of support, nor do they have the *means* to be your sole emotional support system. Yet they will be some of your most important coaches—a person who you can trust to tell you what you need to hear when you need it the most.

> During the most stressful times, it is so important to keep the ones that are closest to you *close to you* and not just give up.

A CHANGE OF SEASONS ...

Once the kids went off to college, for the first time in a long, long time, it was more about us. I continued my leadership journey and Kathy went back to work to have a successful engineering career.

There were some challenging days, but my wife and kids were a big part of helping me on my journey.

Leadership and life are a process of constant, lifelong change, with many challenges along the way. You cannot go on that journey alone.

Coaches

I talked earlier about getting yourself a coach. The reality is that we need *many* coaches. My greatest coach, who has been there the whole time, is my wife, Kathy, of course. She has been there with me and *for me* through my entire working career and through all the experiences you've read about in this book.

The psychiatrist and psychologist who helped me out of my depression were also great coaches. They helped me see life in a much broader way.

Another is a great friend, Phil, who has been there for me, just as I hope I've been there for him for many years.

Even my kids have listened to my challenges and helped me view things in another light from time to time. All three are millennials (they hate it when I call them that). They helped me understand how the next generation thinks and that what you hear from consultants and read in books isn't totally accurate. They coached me well in understanding what's important to the next generation: respect, opportunities to grow, a boss and company who care about them and appreciate their contributions. They want to be taught and mentored in the path forward and have a good work-life balance. Sound familiar? Who is that *not* important to?

An example of how my grown children affected my thinking was the feedback I heard from them regarding rigid corporate structures—often the kinds of corporate structures that are recommended by management consultants. They talked about how easy it was for them to feel completely removed from the leadership of the company. While the company might issue all the "correct" platitudes, they never felt *heard*. This kind of feedback inspired me to start a new program called **Chat with Pat**, where I engaged personally with each group and office within the company.

It was a forum where all, from the newest of employees to the old guard, felt free to ask whatever questions they wanted to of me—and ask they did. I knew we had created a comfortable environment, because of how challenging the questions were and the fact that they came from all tiers within the organization.

Another coach for many years was Susie, who was our company's entire human resources team in the early years. Susie has a greater understanding of people than anyone I know. She always knew the right thing to do when dealing with "people issues." I felt like I had empathy for people, but not as much as I really needed. Susie helped me keep my focus on business in check, to remember that it's *about the people.* She helped me understand how decisions we were contemplating would be viewed by the employees, and how those decisions would affect the people of the firm. She was and continues to be instrumental in defining and maintaining the people-first culture.

A number of years ago, I joined a group that consisted of CEOs (about sixteen of us) from companies in all different types of businesses, large and small. We met once a month to talk about and vet issues—issues that we really could not talk about to those within our company. What I discovered was that virtually all leaders deal with the same issues, just on a different scale. *The issues are almost always about people, relationships, stress*—how people react to that stress and how people interact with one another. That group became another form of coaching for me.

COACH DENNIS

Dennis, the leader of the group, became a good friend and one of my closest coaches. He was my *personal executive coach*. Dennis had an incredible ability to ask tough questions about the issue at hand to help me think with greater depth and breadth so I could consider all options. Those hard questions he asked often made me feel uncomfortable, and I sometimes resented the inquisition. In retrospect, the exercise was healthy and *necessary to uncover my blind spots* and make me look inwardly at how I was contributing to company issues. That CEO group, and Dennis, helped me to think more deeply about how to address the challenges with the office leader that I spoke of earlier. They held me accountable to work on that issue until a solution was found. Without them, I don't know if I would have ever truly solved it. Lesson to be learned here: *Get yourself a coach. No excuses!*

More Than a Coach ...

One of my greatest coaches along the way was much more than a coach. He was a coworker, colleague, fellow leader, friend—and he continues to be a close friend. Roman started work at Halff about a year after I did. We "grew up" together and also joined the management team together in 1997. When I became chief operating officer, he became senior vice president on the management team. We worked together for many years to lead the firm. When I became president in 2013, he became chief operating officer.

We became close confidants to each other. We held each other accountable, tested ideas with each other, and never made an important decision without listening to the other's opinion. He was the ultimate sparring partner. When I use the word "I" throughout this book to describe decisions that were made, I mean "we," *because Roman was always a part of those critical decisions*. I was fortunate to have a person whom I knew and trusted so well and who also trusted me.

> *Leaders need coaches.*

So you see, it's not just one person. *It's a whole team of coaches.* I don't know if you have these people or can develop relationships with people so that they can become coaches for you, but the closer you can get to people, the better you will be in dealing with the challenges that come your way.

Who are your coaches? Are you listening to them? Will they tell you more than just what you want to hear? ***Will they tell you what you* need *to hear?***

Key Takeaways

- Your immediate family will always be along for the ride on your leadership journey. Just like your other coaches, they can provide you with valuable feedback and help you monitor your stress levels and empathy quotients.

- Coaches come in all forms and are necessary partners for your journey. Listen openly, and ask them to hold you accountable.

Call to Action

1. Do you have a worthy sparring partner? In what ways do they challenge you? If you don't have one, find yourself one.

2. Do you have a plan for balancing personal responsibilities with leadership demands? Have a plan for monitoring the success of your plan. Ask for feedback from family members. Communication is key.

3. Do you have coaches? Who are they? If you don't, find some.

CHAPTER 7

GROWTH

Without continual growth and progress, such words as improvement, achievement, and success have no meaning.
—BENJAMIN FRANKLIN

Personal Growth

A LITTLE STORY ABOUT WHAT HAPPENS IN LIFE

Leadership requires constant growth. After I began to heal from the traumatic events of 2017, I decided that I *did* want to step down as the president of the company. I wanted to step away from all the stress before I was too old to enjoy some of the fruits of my labor.

I stepped down as president and off the management team at the end of 2019, but I continued to work part time on initiatives that I enjoyed—things that could bring value to current and next-generation leaders. I was moving into the next phase of my life and feeling good about this upcoming season when I was hit with a surprise.

While on a business trip in Florida, I began to see a thin brown streak in the upper corner of my right eye one Thursday evening. When I woke up Friday morning, the streak had become a curtain, slowly closing in on my vision. I decided I'd better go see an eye doctor. The doctor took one look at my eye and said, "You're going to see a retina specialist right now."

The retina specialist, after a quick exam, said, "It's retina surgery for you, bud, and you aren't going anywhere until that's done." After the unexpected, unplanned, emergency retina surgery, the next bit of news was, "You aren't traveling anywhere for a week. Enjoy your stay in Tallahassee!"

So there I was, stuck in Florida for a week. Well, I must admit there are worse places in the world to be stuck. My wife joined me for the surgery and several days after. She returned home, and my son came to stay with me for a quickly planned minivacation in Sandestin.

Why am I telling you all this?

Because this is a little story about what happens in life. ***There are twists and turns, ups and downs—just like in business. We have no control over them.*** The only thing we can control is how we react to those twists and turns. So when life takes control, what are you going to do? Get angry? Get upset? Are you going to let a change of plans or a setback in your grand plan ruin your day, or will you make the most of it?

I NOW HAVE BETTER VISION—FIGURATIVELY AND LITERALLY!

This event was another reminder that we really are not in control of as much as we think we are. Plans change, whether we like it or not. I could have been on the plane, heading somewhere and needing serious surgery and not able to get it done. I could have gone blind in one eye. Life always has a funny way of ironing things out. *How we react to those twists and turns has a major impact on what the outcome will be.*

My wife, son, and I ended up having one of the best, most relaxing vacations we've ever had. There was no pressure about what had to be done at that moment, no stress about what we had to do next. I got to relax, recover, and chill out for a few days. In previous times, holidays and vacations were always prefaced with a greater amount of stress at work. I could not get into "paradise mode." I would stay in problem-solving mode. That week, I had a greater appreciation for my family, my health, and my free time.

This is one of the main reasons I decided to write this book. I wanted to help people reflect and think about how the challenging days affect their lives. I wanted to share some tips and personal lessons about how to turn those challenging days into days for growth and positive outcomes. Instead of the *difficult events in my life* breaking me (surgery after surgery, ruined plans, leaving my position as president), they *became only temporary setbacks, and ultimately catalysts for me to heal and grow*. They encouraged me to get better, start fresh, have better vision. I now have better vision— figuratively and literally!

> When life takes control, what are you going to do? Get angry? Get upset? Are you going to let a change of plans or a setback in your grand plan ruin your day, or will you make the most of it?

I WAS GOING IN THE WRONG DIRECTION AND AWAY FROM MY PURPOSE ...

In general, I have taken these challenging moments in stride and moved on. Something like a detached retina would have me say, "If it can be fixed, fix it and go on." Looking back to those times when I was at my highest stress level, I did not realize that, at some point, I had stopped handling things this way. I would let things that happened and other inconveniences get to me. I didn't have the same energy to let things go.

I was going in the wrong direction and away from my purpose— not really understanding or thinking about what my purpose was. I didn't realize how much stress and disconnection had built up until I stepped away from it.

After my eye healed, *I went back to work with a renewed sense of self.* It was a night-and-day difference. There was no stress. I came home to my family and said to any of the household problems, "OK, we will figure it out," with complete ease. This became a monumental step in my growth as a person. However, it happened late in my career!

My hope is that this book causes you to think about what your purpose is and where you are headed, before something unexpected or even catastrophic happens to you. Perhaps sharing my experiences can lessen the learning curve for others.

Growth is like climate. You need to adjust and adapt to situations—wherever you are. You might think getting to the top—in business, personal wealth and society—is a measure of success. Those are merely trophies. *True growth is horizontal.* You need to see the world around you, at your level, at this moment in time, and grow as a person first. What does this truly mean?

Here's what I learned after those traumatic moments in my life: my immediate task had to be **_working on myself first_** to change how I viewed and approached the world around me. Evaluate where you are from time to time, essentially instituting checkpoints in your life line. If you are not headed in the right direction, make a commitment to adjust your direction—and stick to your commitment.

So how will you react when that life-changing event interrupts your business or personal life? What decisions will you make?

It could be an event that you are fortunate enough to live through, such as a heart attack, experiencing the grief of losing a loved one, or some major decision that could have a dramatic impact on the rest of your life. There is always the possibility of a setback. If you are fortunate that it hasn't happened in your life _yet_, then look around you and see what is happening. Take a glance at people you know who have health issues or at that executive who died because of this or that. You'll quickly realize **_no one is bulletproof._**

You could have a zillion dollars dropped into your bank account after a successful business deal—then be diagnosed with cancer the next day. Steve Jobs is an example of a man who seemingly had it all—at least everything money could buy—yet his life was cut unexpectedly short when he succumbed to cancer at the age of fifty-six. Life is ephemeral and mysterious. Nobody knows tomorrow. This is the beauty of changing how we think, behave, and act in the now. ***Good leaders know that challenges will come and that learning to deal with them in a positive way is a* process.** Wintley Phipps said it well: "Son, if the mountain were smooth, you couldn't climb it." No matter the outcome or risk, challenges and changes in our lives can be a good thing or a bad thing (or maybe some of both)—depending on how we react to them. You, and *only you*, decide how you will grow, during and after the challenges and changes that will occur in your life.

> **You get to decide whether the challenges and changes you face will be a good thing or a bad thing. It was Shakespeare who said, "'Tis an ill wind that blows no good." You decide.**

Corporate Growth

Remember, growth was essential for our firm to reach its overarching goal: personal and professional growth for everyone. But it's even more basic than that. There's an old saying: ***"If you're not growing, you're dying."*** I think that's true. Why do you want to grow? Who is excited about going to work and doing the same thing year after year for the next twenty years? A company that offers only that experience isn't growing.

That hits home for me. ***Lack of growth isn't fun or exciting.*** If you don't grow, you're going to be flat. When you are flat, you'll soon begin to lose the edge and go downhill. That, I know, is painful. Nobody says that's why they grow, but it's a big part of it.

The philosophy that we consistently conveyed to our employees to drive growth was that if you focus on doing the right things— having a sense of ownership in everything you do, treating people with respect, taking care of your clients, etc.—everything else will fall into place. The firm's financial metrics will take care of themselves: you are going to be profitable, revenue will increase, there will be growth opportunities, stock price will rise—precisely because **you are** doing the right things. You're training and mentoring your people and giving them the tools, the opportunity, and the autonomy to succeed. And in turn the firm will succeed.

When we make good profits, people will get a good solid compensation package. When we make those good profits, there will be opportunities to invest in growth, such as new business lines, new offices, and mergers and acquisitions. This growth will result in opportunities for each employee to personally participate in that growth. That was the philosophy. This was no "Which comes first, the chicken or the egg?" conundrum—we **knew** what came first—***doing the right things!***

When everyone is on board with this philosophy, I believe then and only then can a firm truly reach its greatest potential. I believe that we were closest to this from 2013 to 2019. This can clearly be seen when you look at some of the performance metrics for the firm during this time period compared to previous periods. Our strategy was working for *everyone.* During that period, we experienced unprecedented growth in revenue, profit, and stock value—and grew from roughly four hundred to almost one thousand employees.

Focused, Flexible Growth

AVOIDING "SHINY OBJECT SYNDROME"

No question, you must be laser focused on the reason why you want growth and the plan that will get you there. But you also need to be flexible. Those attributes seem like opposites, but it is *important to have both focus and flexibility*. You must be ready to change the plan's direction if the circumstances require it, without falling prey to "shiny object syndrome." That's where *everything* seems like a great opportunity, and focus is lost. Yet without flexibility, you will find yourself on a treadmill, obsessed with chasing the plan when circumstances have changed, and the plan won't work!

Leaders must ask questions of themselves *and* of the organization. Then they must be ready to dive deep into the resulting answers and ideas. *The most important question any organization and its leader must ask is, "What are we trying to achieve?"* The answer to that question should be something that will not change over time.

Then you must stay focused to achieve that overarching goal. One of the things I said to myself all the time was, "Don't take your eye off the goal." *If you have honestly answered the question of what you are trying to achieve, then being clear about the goal should be simple.* But let's face it; it's not that simple! The goal may stay the same, but the plan needs to change as necessary to accomplish the goal.

The world around us changes constantly. It's easy to get distracted and lose sight of what we are trying to accomplish. For example, everyone faced trying times throughout the pandemic of 2020, and it was easy to get distracted. Offices were shut down, businesses closed, and kids stayed home for remote learning and homeschooling. What a challenging time! The pandemic, ongoing as I write, continues to be a trying time for everyone. And it is a time none of us will ever forget. We need to step back, refocus on what our goals are now, and make sure we are still headed in the right direction as we define it.

Focus for leaders is essential, especially during a crisis. I am a spontaneous person by nature. I could wake up today and be totally focused on something, then wake up tomorrow and say, "Well, this is boring," and move on to something totally different. Are you anything like that? It's a common trait of entrepreneurs. *If you find that your focus shifts from day to day, it's time to ask yourself and your organization if what you are focusing on right now is going to help you achieve your goals.*

In retrospect, I thought I had a pretty clear vision, but I often found myself going off on tangents and temporarily losing sight of the primary objective.

WORK IN OUR INDUSTRY CHANGED

I felt I had a clear vision of building a firm where people could grow in their careers and find long-term personal and professional job satisfaction. But that vision became blurred when work in our industry changed. For years we performed under a model in which we worked directly for project owners. Those owners continued to have follow-up projects, and with that model, we were able to build a sustainable workload and workforce to perform services for those clients. That model allowed us to build long-term relationships with our clients and have a sustained workflow upon which we could hire and provide long-term and sustained career opportunities for people.

Along came a new procurement model—design-build—in which project owners hired a construction contractor or financier to lead large projects. In this model, a firm would work for that project lead, one step removed from the owner. The project lead would not necessarily have a continuous flow of projects. So the firm would potentially win a project and have to staff up for it. When that project was finished, staff layoffs would have to occur, letting people go who were hired to perform the work for that project.

We saw this shift, this new way of doing business. What we saw was the potential for more work, more revenue and profits from these types of projects, and we chased those projects hard. We invested significantly to pursue and win those projects.

We won a few, performed that work, then realized what it meant: *hiring and firing for a specific project—one and done—which is in direct conflict with our overarching goal of building and growing people's careers!* After a significant financial investment and difficult layoffs, we realized this was the wrong direction. It wasn't consistent with our culture and core values, and we would never truly be successful with it because of this inconsistency.

> *If it's not ultimately getting you closer to the primary objective, then why are you spending time on it?*

It can happen throughout an organization. I've been known to pull people aside and say, *"OK, you said you wanted to do this, so why are you doing that instead, and how is it going to help you get where you want to be?"* If it's not ultimately getting you closer to the primary objective, then why are you spending time on it?

THE PURSUIT ...

For example, one of the strongest practices at our company had been floodplain/flood analysis and watershed management. There was so much of this work in Texas and in the other states where we had offices. One of our primary growth strategies was to grow that practice in the areas where we had a strong presence.

There was plenty of work, and we were well positioned to reach our growth objectives in those regions. But next thing you know, we began putting all sorts of effort into chasing a watershed management pursuit in another region. So why were we doing that? We had just made a major investment in Florida. We had tremendous opportunities in our current locations. We had said we wanted to grow in the geographic regions where we were located. Yet for some reason, *we took our eye off the goal*.

It was a change from what we had said we were trying to achieve—it spread our resources and our leaders very thin. The leaders of that practice put everything they had into that pursuit and were committed to winning; however, the leaders of the firm were not all on the same page. In retrospect, there was not adequate dialogue between the top leadership of the firm and those engaged in this practice. If there had been dialogue, maybe we, as a whole, would have changed our focus slightly—understood that this opportunity was too great to pass up—and the firm could perhaps have put more resources into the pursuit to win. One could argue that it was a waste of energy, because without real focus from top leadership of the firm on down—without everyone on the same page—we didn't do all that we might have done to win that project. We chased a major project, put significant investment into winning that project, and lost.

You will not be successful if you chase tangential shiny pennies, where everyone is not on the same page working together to achieve the objective. Why? Because the passion is not there at all levels of the organization, and you won't do everything you can—internally and externally—to win. This is true at all levels, no matter how large or small the goal you are chasing, no matter whether it is another project, another client, or starting a business as an entrepreneur.

Now to the final chapter of that lost pursuit. To the credit of our leaders in that practice, they saw opportunities and made the case that we had to be flexible. *We had to change the plan.* This was the kind of work that is *consistent with our culture, who we are as a firm*—and the work that would help us meet our primary goals. They didn't give up. We chased the next major project, with everyone aligned, and won! Yes, stay focused, but remain flexible.

Even if the opportunity seems amazing, you can't chase every shiny penny. You can't put your best foot forward to win everything; you will become distracted and lose sight of your primary goal. That doesn't mean you should say no to everything that comes along that doesn't fit the plan exactly. But if the opportunity doesn't meet the overarching goal of what you are trying to achieve as a firm, don't waste your time with it.

Keep your eye on the proverbial ball! Do you really want to chase every shiny object and then, in a few years, wonder, "Well, how come we didn't reach our goals?" Everything must revolve around the firm's primary goals. *There should be only one, two, or three goals you're trying to achieve*, and everything else should support those primary objectives. It's as simple as this: if an organization has a goal in mind, but the majority of its programs do not relate to that goal, then the organization and the people within that organization are just being distracted.

If you, as a leader, entrepreneur, or small business owner, want to grow, stay focused on what that growth looks like and why it is critical. On the flip side, *we can become obsessed with growth to the point where it becomes a detriment* to us, to our family, to our firm, or even to the ability to achieve success itself. Don't let that happen!

Constant laser focus is difficult to maintain. Keeping your focus in the right direction is even harder. Take time to pause and think about the things you've got to do. Recalibrate. Stay on track.

Risk and Change

Growth is fun and rewarding, but it can also be uncomfortable. Growth means change, and taking risks that can be stressful. That's OK. It's exciting. It's challenging. You see people getting excited about growing and doing new things. You also get to do and see new things. ***But with growth comes change, and it means taking risk—uncomfortable risk.***

For leaders to be successful, they must be willing to take on risk. They need to embrace change. They must be able to be *change agents* and convince the people of the firm that change is good—and that everyone will reap the benefits. But how do you convey change to all employees so it will be embraced and accepted? That can be very difficult.

CONNECT THE DOTS ...

Some people settle in and are comfortable doing the same things over and over again, day after day. You personally can be very comfortable; everything is working right in your world. However, to achieve growth, the leader must embrace change and sell the benefits of change and growth. Leaders must connect the dots for people and be able to articulate that the risk is reasonable, won't cause too much disruption, and, if successful, will contribute to the firm's primary objectives and to each individual's aspirations.

Growing companies have to be willing to take risks and make decisions to do something bold. When you make those decisions, the feeling of dread and fear can take over at first. You might think, "Everything we have could crumble if this doesn't work." But once you take that step and see the positive excitement from people following that decision—seeing small successes—you can actually feel the adrenaline that comes from them bringing it to life. Think of a time when you left your comfort zone and took a risk—when everything turned out well, and you and others around you saw success and growth. How did that feel at the start of that endeavor versus months later, when objectives were achieved?

It is imperative that the firm's leaders are on the same page when it comes to taking risks. *Everyone's risk tolerance is different*, so there has to be dialogue and discussion to understand the risk tolerance of the leaders involved in the endeavor. *Hash out why the risk is being taken, the potential positive outcomes, and the potential downside of the endeavor if it goes wrong, so that everyone can get comfortable with taking the risk and support moving forward.* Without that conversation and without the leaders involved in the initiatives being comfortable with the potential risk, the endeavor will be doomed.

ANALYSIS PARALYSIS ...

No problem can withstand the assault of sustained thinking.
—VOLTAIRE

For years, we said we wanted to grow. To do that, we wanted to embark on acquisitions of firms to complement our core business. We found, met with, evaluated, and analyzed many firms—good firms that checked all the boxes related to how we wanted to grow. Yet somehow, we found a way to overanalyze and create questions that were so detailed that each of the potential acquisitions failed for one reason or another.

One firm on which we spent considerable time was a small firm that conducted flood analysis for rivers and streams (one of our core business areas). It was located in a city where we wanted to grow. The leader wanted to sell, but he cared immensely about his people and wanted to make sure they were taken care of, which was consistent with our core values. The firm also had a great reputation in the marketplace for doing quality work—also consistent with our core values. The firm checked all the boxes—their operating philosophy, culture, and core values were consistent with ours. Yet we found a way to overanalyze the financials—kept asking questions about their client base and performance—to the point where the leader of the firm walked away from the deal.

There are no risk-free deals! We said we wanted to acquire firms, but collectively we—the management team and board of directors—were not on the same page with how much risk we could accept, so we kept asking questions until the deal finally died. This happened with multiple potential deals.

It was not until we took the time to openly discuss the risk associated with acquisitions that we were able to embark on a robust

135

acquisition program. We created what-if scenarios with hypothetical deals, showing what the potential downside would be if a deal went south and, conversely, showing what the upside would be if the deal worked well. That process was followed by candid, open conversations about what risk we, as leaders, were willing to take. Leaders must be on the same page to be successful. If not, they can talk themselves out of anything. And remember, as hockey-hall-of-famer Wayne Gretzky said, "You miss 100 percent of the shots you don't take!"

> **Never look back after the decision is made.
> It's a new day.**

Risk-taking is almost like a drug—it can be addictive. But don't take risks unless the reasons and the objectives for taking them are clear. You must have a specific goal in mind to get anywhere. To reach that goal, you need to have a reason—a cause to change.

People have asked me, "How did you make those bigger decisions at your company and take those risks?" The reality is that I never viewed the decisions I made as major risks. I saw them as decisions that had to be made after careful thought and consideration. I knew that every decision had its consequences. Some of the greatest stresses for me came in the middle of making decisions—wanting to make the right decisions, knowing there would be positives and negatives. I wanted to make a decision that I would be at peace with, one whose consequences I could live with. But once the decision was made, I never looked back.

As you grow and climb further in your leadership journey, the decisions become more and more gray. Most often, there is no clear right or wrong. One path may be better than another, but still there is no clear right or wrong. The success or failure of the decision is determined by how it is implemented and managed. Never look back after your decision is made. It's a new day and a time to work on moving forward, not to look back.

SUMMING IT UP ...

In 2013, I became president of the firm. We had just recovered from the economic downturn, and I could have said, "You know what, I only have six or seven years left before I retire. I don't need to take these risks anymore. I could just ride out my time, be stable, and it will all be good." But where's the fun in that? Why go to work every day if that's all it is? As I said earlier, I am driven by people—watching and helping people grow. In turn, growing a company means people need to have the opportunities to grow. That's what motivates me.

I am motivated much more by the desire and excitement of growth than by money. Am I going to be happy doing the same thing day after day? Probably not. I can't say that I wake up jumping for joy every day, but when I wake up, my mind does begin working on different things to do than I did the day before.

What motivates me to get up and get moving in the morning is to be able to touch people's lives in a positive way. I love knowing that I can focus my energy on doing something meaningful that will have a positive impact on the lives of the people whom I touch. That's what growth is about for me, and that's what justifies the risk and the discomfort that comes with it.

Key Takeaways

- "'Tis an ill wind that blows no good." In the midst of the storm, reflect to find the good, and carry forward lessons learned.

- Focus on doing the right things and let the pieces come together for a successful outcome. Right things often begin with the word *respect*: respect for people, respect for company values, respect for clients, etc.

- Growth provides excitement and fulfillment but always requires risk. Keep your eye on the prize, determine a level of acceptable risk, and strive to find that elusive sweet spot between "ready, fire, aim" and "analysis paralysis."

- Once you make a critical decision, don't look back.

Call to Action

1. Reflect on your purpose—What actions have you taken recently that are consistent with your purpose? What actions have you taken recently that are deflecting from, distracting from, or destroying your purpose?

2. Analyze your risk tolerance. What tangible measures can you use to assess what is an acceptable level of risk for your organization?

3. Wherever you are on the risk spectrum, seek feedback from others, especially those with expertise outside your comfort zone (financial, marketing, legal, etc.).

CHAPTER 8

SUCCESS

Define success on your own terms ... and
build a life you're proud to live.
—ANNE SWEENEY

What Does Success Mean?

How do you define success? If you haven't stopped to ask yourself that question, maybe you should. Sometimes we get so busy with the day-to-day challenges of life that we forget what we are working toward.

It took me years to get off the hectic work treadmill, and if I had not had a traumatic health crisis, I might not have gotten off at all. ***It's easy to lose touch with what makes you happy when you're busy running a company or you're so focused on results.*** I've seen executives, entrepreneurs, and leaders at all levels lose sight of what makes them happy. As a result, they lost sight of what it takes to be a successful leader too. Having a place to think, a retreat, helped me realize what success would look like for me. As I asked you in an earlier chapter, where is your retreat? What does your getaway look like?

what does success
look like to you?

No matter where you are at this point in your life, take time to pause and think about why you're in the role you're in and if you even enjoy the work you do. There are lots of people who just chase a paycheck and lack joy or passion at work. They just go through the motions, and they act out in anger and feel stressed because they're never really fulfilled.

Wherever you are now doesn't have to be where you are in the future. You can move, make a change, switch careers. Too many times, people get stuck in a comfort zone and live with unnecessary stress. They lack meaning or purpose in their jobs and lives for years.

When you're focused on the bottom line, you can lose touch with what's important to you and what it means to be a leader. Leaders have to be focused on achieving the results that their boss wants, and most often that means focusing on the bottom-line financial performance of the company. But in the end, will that buy you success? What really drives you? What motivates you? I would argue that *for most people, if they have searched deep enough, they will realize that financial achievements are really only a means to an end.* They will find that true success is far more complex than just how much profit was earned by the firm this year—or how much money they made personally.

For me, it was about people and focusing on people first. What is it for you? Many things will factor into how you define success.

Coaches are so important in helping you understand what really drives you and evaluate whether you are working toward your personal inner passions. Those coaches will also help keep you grounded. Leaders have made it to the top because they did some things right. And along the way, they have gained tremendous confidence in themselves. *But remember the saying: "What got you here won't get you there."*

Having confidence is a good thing, but it can also work against you. If you think you are always right, you will not make the best decisions; no one is always right. *By definition, you are unaware of your blind spots.* Only a coach can help you take a step back, look at yourself, and view the things around you differently. This can be very powerful; it will help you make better decisions. It will make you a better leader.

SUCCESSFUL DECISION-MAKING …

If you are going to be an effective leader, you have to be able to articulate why you make certain decisions in a way that people will buy into them. Effective leaders have a clear understanding of what they are trying to accomplish, which allows them to communicate their vision and the reasons why decisions are being made. If you can't tell people the why of decision-making, they will lose confidence in you as a leader and make up their own story. And most of the time, that story won't be anywhere close to the truth, and people will not be working together toward a common goal. Drama and a lack of focus will prevail, making it very difficult for the firm to achieve success. So be transparent and tell the truth about why certain decisions are made. People might not like or agree with your decisions, but the transparency and honesty you portray will build incredible trust and loyalty in people.

TRANSPARENCY TO THE RESCUE ...

For many years, our firm had no specific maternity policy or benefits. It was not common in our industry at that time, and if we had initiated one, it would have been funded by the profits of the firm—the profit that was used to compensate people in the form of end-of-the-year bonuses. Many would have viewed it as providing a benefit to a specific demographic in the firm while diminishing employee compensation for some, which, at the time, we had determined was not in the best interest of the people of the firm as a whole.

This, as you can imagine, was a very controversial topic. Some people did not like the reason why we had no maternity policy—but it was the truth for where we were at the time. While many did not like this policy, it was at least accepted because I discussed it openly in meetings, did not avoid the subject, and—most importantly—told the truth rather than avoiding the topic or having some generic response that didn't actually address the topic. We did, however, also state that, at some point in time, it would become more standard in the industry, and there would no doubt be such a benefit—and in fact, there did come a day when a maternity, and even more inclusive paternity leave benefit program was instituted.

Had I not addressed this head-on, people would have made up a story, something like "They don't respect or support family like they say they do" or "The leaders are just cheap—don't want to spend the money—they want to keep the money for themselves and just pay themselves more. They don't care about the employees."

I believe that not addressing important issues will erode the trust and confidence people have in their leaders. It was crucial to keep the employees informed on matters of employee compensation! It's important to address sensitive and difficult topics openly—and always tell the truth.

If you can't tell people the why of decision-making, they will lose confidence in you as a leader. Effective leaders must have frequent, open communication about the decisions being made.

It is imperative to ***keep the next-generation leaders close to you***. Communicate with them regularly so they understand why you are making the decisions you are making. Clearly articulate how those decisions are aligned with the vision and direction of the firm. This will result in clarity and consistency and ultimately in achieving success for the firm, its people, and for the leaders personally. If they understand why the decision was made and the thought and effort that went into that decision—even if they don't completely agree with it—they can and will be your greatest supporters. If you don't take the time, and they don't understand, they will be your greatest roadblock to success.

Have you ever been part of an organization, maybe a social or community organization, in which decisions were handed down from "on high," and no explanation or transparency was ever provided? How apt were you to want to embrace a strategy presented in this way, especially when you didn't understand the logic of it and weren't allowed to ask questions?

WAS IT WORTH IT?

Money can't buy happiness. Or can it? Maybe it can buy vacations and boats but not true fulfillment. Why do I think this? Because I see people who have a lot of wealth, and many of their lives are in turmoil.

I got to the top step, and I ask myself repeatedly whether it was worth it. I think what made it worth it for me was to see the people's lives I touched, the people whom I helped to achieve goals along the way.

When you go to work for a firm—and even more importantly, if you grow to the point in which you are a leader at some level in the firm—it is *imperative that the firm's core values fit your personal values* and align with your vision. If this alignment does not exist, you're never going to be happy, and it will also be much more difficult for you to lead the firm to success.

I truly cared about people when I became president. But I can't say that I was aware of it at the time. In retrospect, I did some things that were not consistent with that. And had I known what I know

now, I would change some of the decisions I made and how I behaved in some instances.

Many times I said, "My job would be a lot easier if it weren't for all the damned people!" Quite ironic since that is exactly what my job was—managing the people! Without the people, I would have no job either. That attitude was so inconsistent with what truly drove me— helping people build their careers. *I wonder how much better my life would have been and how much more successful of an organization we could have been if I had understood myself better years ago.* I realize now that it was always very important to me to treat people right and that it was my personal core value in all that I did.

WHAT YOU SAY AND WHAT YOU DO MUST BE CONSISTENT

So if this is all true, considering some of the leaders that came before me (those I talked about earlier), how did I stay at this company for so long? Why did I stay if they were so different from me? The truth is that I believe they had many of the same deep inner-core values that I have. I believe they also embraced many of the same core values as Dr. Halff; they cared about the people within the firm, wanted to help the employees grow in their careers, and wanted to treat all employees with respect. But within the firm, their actions created a perception that was different from their beliefs and objectives. They didn't see it. They didn't surround themselves with people who could point out their blind spots—people whom they trusted, who saw things differently than they did, and whom they would listen to.

They did, however, hire good people with values similar to mine. They built a successful firm in a lot of ways—a very stable firm. But I would argue that *the firm never reached its greatest potential because of their inability to see their blind spots.* Had they understood how their actions were inconsistent with their own core values and the impact that had on people, and had they been able to change the way they worked with people, the firm could have harnessed their energy and their passion and could have had even greater success than it did.

In the end, to be successful, your personal values and what you are passionate about must align with the culture and goals of the firm. Your blind spots can cause you to take actions that are inconsistent with those values. Understand what drives you, and acknowledge your blind spots. If you can manage them and focus on what really motivates you, you'll find more success as a leader.

It is also important that your communication about what the firm is trying to achieve is consistent. That can only happen if you are truly passionate about the vision and goals.

What am I passionate about? People growing in their careers. We had a strategic plan that said we wanted to grow 10 to 15 percent per year. I wanted to bring in more key hires—people who could bring in new clients and opportunities—and I wanted to keep hiring more and more younger people. *The concept was that continuous growth—bringing in new clients, new opportunities, and more revenue—would result in career growth for everyone.* At the same time, it was every bit as important to me to ensure we were building upon the people-first culture that our founder, Dr. Halff, had originally created. I tried to repeat that message in every presentation and conversation with everyone I spoke to, in one way or another.

YOUR MESSAGE MUST BE CONSISTENT, OVER AND OVER AGAIN ...

So if your goal is to build a people-first firm, how do you tie that back to every employee in the firm—the person who is there every day giving it their all? The aphorism that "there is no *I* in *team*" proves itself in real life. How do you articulate that in a way that everyone sees and understands? You can get the top leaders to buy in, to a certain extent, but how do you bring the message to the rest of the employees so that they truly buy into it, believe it, and benefit from it? How do you get that message to everyone in the firm when you have to keep focused on the business and profitability? Whatever it is that you do—your actions, your initiatives, what you say—be honest and true. Your message must be consistent and must be repeated over and over again.

I'm passionate about treating people with respect and giving them opportunities to grow. For me, that had to be at the core of the strategic plan. For example, if I want to add offices or invest in new key hires or new technology, *I can and must clearly articulate why we are pursuing these objectives and how they can result in growth for the firm and career-growth opportunities for the individual*. By being sincere in my actions, people could always see I wanted to help the firm grow and build sustainable success, which was needed for the personal growth and job and financial stability for each individual at the company. It was not just in my words but in my actions and everything I did. That's why the people, and ultimately the firm, were successful.

> **Define your vision ... articulate it ...
> communicate it—consistently.**

Yes, we made profit. Yes, it resulted in greater stock value. Yes, I and others benefited from that. And yes, it gave me and others in the firm personal financial stability. But those were only trophies. The real success for me was seeing the people within the firm grow. To quote author and motivational speaker Zig Ziglar, "You don't build a business. You build people, and people build the business." That quote sums it up well for me and what I am about and what I worked to bring to the organization.

If, at the heart of your strategic plan, the goal is not *taking care of people* but rather increasing stock value and personal net worth, you will never be able to articulate the plan in a way that people will buy into.

I could explain to people why I was trying to grow the firm. I could tell people that my compensation, like everyone else's, was tied to my individual performance. ***All the firm's profit was distributed to the people based on performance, with no correlation to ownership.***

The conversation could then easily follow with the benefits to each individual: "When we grow as a company, here is what that means to you, how you can grow in your career, how you can take your career to the next level. You can also own stock, gain greater financial rewards, and benefit from stock growth—all based on your contribution to the firm's success." Those statements and the references to stock had real meaning, because as I said earlier, common stock was broadly held (over three hundred shareholders today), and in fact, everyone owned stock through the employee stock ownership plan.

The ability to put those pieces together in a visionary plan—one that you can articulate—of how employees can benefit will result in your employees' understanding and belief in it and you. Because it's the truth: *everyone* is included.

> **Articulate how profit and growth goals benefit all employees.**

On the other hand, if your plan is summarized this way: *"The leaders decided where we want to take the company, and this will be really good because, at the end of the day, it will increase our profits and stock value, resulting in happy shareholders and investors."* That's all fine and good, but how do you take that message to employees and inspire them? There must be a deeper reason for why you're doing it rather than just to increase profits for shareholders. If you can define that deeper reason, connect it to the goals and initiatives your company has set, and tie that to the goals and lives of all employees, your chance of truly reaching success—for you and your company—will increase dramatically.

Key Takeaways

- The success of the organization is dependent upon your personal goals and values aligning with the culture, goals, and values of the company.

- As wise man Louis Brandeis once said, "Sunlight is said to be the best disinfectant." Transparency in decision-making is a must, as it will prevent the germination of distrust.

- ***Don't just talk the talk; walk the walk.*** So simple, yet so easy to forget. The importance of this age-old truism should never be underestimated in a leader's journey.

Call to Action

1. Reflect on what success means to you.

2. Understand your own passion, and build a vision for the firm that is consistent with that passion. ***Define your vision*** in a

clear message to the people of your company. *Articulate it* in an honest and transparent way. And *communicate it—consistently*, over and over again. That's how you'll find success.

CHAPTER 9

LEADERSHIP JOURNEY

Leadership development is a lifetime journey, not a quick trip.
—JOHN C. MAXWELL

Ownership

To build a firm that reaches its greatest potential, people need to feel as though they are truly a part of it. How do you accomplish that? ***By creating a company where the people have a piece of the pie—some level of ownership in the firm.***

A DECISION TO BROADEN OWNERSHIP

When our founder, Dr. Halff, first sold the company, we had about one hundred employees and fifteen shareholders. He was a firm believer in the concept that ownership results in great success. After he sold the firm, it grew modestly, but the number of shareholders did not. Later, when the decision was made to broaden ownership, the firm picked up momentum, and we could see greater success in reaching our goals for growth.

I believe there is a direct correlation between ownership and success of the firm. It all revolves around key people and leaders and their sense of ownership, their drive to succeed for the good of the company. ***Entrepreneurs or owners are often reluctant to give the next generation of leaders the opportunity to own stock***—understandably so, because they took the risks and poured themselves into creating and building the firm in the first place. Who wants to *give* that away? Well, maybe there's more to it than the value of the firm. Maybe there's something more important, such as a deeper sense of purpose for the owner. Maybe building people is just as important (or more important) than financial gain.

AN INVESTMENT IN PEOPLE THAT PAYS OFF

On top of that, I believe and have witnessed that the investment made by *giving* people stock—ownership—pays off in growth of the firm. The resulting increase in stock value, due to the renewed sense of energy, passion, and desire to make the firm succeed, permeates throughout the firm by the new next-generation owners. In short, there are two great benefits to the current owners from expanding ownership: (1) the ability to see *people grow and flourish in their careers* and (2) *greater financial rewards* from increased growth and the resulting increased stock value, driven in part by people's opportunity to participate as owners in the firm.

A GIFT, NOT A PURCHASE ...

I have used the term *given* several times. What do I mean by that? I have heard many original owners say, "I give people the opportunity to buy stock, but they just won't buy any," for one reason or another. The fact is that most potential next-generation owners don't have the same risk tolerance as the original owner or entrepreneur who started the firm. They can't stomach buying and taking on the debt and risk. That doesn't necessarily mean they aren't committed or loyal to the firm.

If you really want people to own stock, you must give it to them, at least partially. How? Share the profits—look at it like an investment. *Allow the buyers to share in some of the profits—in the form of compensation, maybe a bonus—and let them use that profit to buy your stock.* Somehow, help the buyers find a way, financially, to own stock. It works. You will receive a return on that investment financially and emotionally as the firm flourishes and grows and as you watch those people stay and grow with you. For me, the latter is the true reward. It's satisfying when you're getting close to retirement and you look back and wonder how you did. Was I successful? I hope you can say, "Yes, I reached my financial goals, but you know what, I also helped some other people get there along the way."

Leadership Tools

TRENDS AND TAGLINES …

Management consultants, supported by various studies and reports over the years, have given leaders concepts, methods, and tools to get people on board with what leadership is trying to accomplish. ***Different philosophies and techniques become the trend of the day, and they come and go.*** It's a vision statement; a mission statement; a definition of values; a purpose statement; a clear definition of your culture; a strategic plan; taglines, big, hairy, audacious goals (BHAGs) … you get the idea.

Take a glance over the last twenty to thirty years, and you'll see it. Today, it's all about having a purpose statement. All these are tools, attempts to give leaders resources to motivate, inspire, and get employees to buy into what is best for the company, why the company exists, and what the goals are moving forward.

The statements by themselves don't work. The passion, heart, and soul of the leader who truly believes in those statements and what they represent will ultimately result in their success for everyone. And the ability of the leader to articulate what those statements mean repeatedly and consistently will make them more impactful. These statements work, more or less, regardless of how passionate the leader is when times are good, there's plenty of work, and everyone is doing well. It's when times get tough that the tools and passion are tested.

> **The actions you take in the difficult moments are what everyone will see and remember.**

When the downturn comes, when the crisis hits—that's when you as a leader get tested on whether or not you truly believe in what these tools represent. Or when something *really* bad happens, and you have to decide between the values, culture, strategic plan, or caring about that person who is working for you versus the bottom line. How are you going to make that decision when the time comes?

The actions you take in the difficult moments are what everyone will see and remember. All the trust and confidence built when things were easy will be wiped away in one misstep during a critical, difficult moment. Those tough times are when you as a leader will be under the most stress, and the tools won't matter. *The decisions you make will be executed based on your personal beliefs and values*—what you are truly passionate about—not on the tools and posters plastered on the walls. If you don't have personal values consistent with the tools, you'll let it slip. You're going to think that you can cover it up, but you can't. These are the times when people are most critical of your behavior and watching your every move.

Take a page from sports: it's not how great an athlete is on his best day; it's how he performs on his worst day. A quarterback can be great on a day when everything is clicking—his performance, the team, the coaches, everything. But how does that quarterback perform on his worst day or when his team is not playing well? Does he choke, or does he rise to the occasion? Does he perform like a leader? Does he still play well enough to win? Does he bring his team together to get through that tough day so the team can still bring home a win?

How do you perform on your or your team's worst day? That's how you will be judged.

Key Takeaways

- Ownership will result in tangible and intangible (financial and personally fulfilling) rewards for all.

- Use management tools from books, podcasts, seminars, etc. judiciously. None of these tools will be effective unless the leader truly believes in them and has passion for them.

- Leadership is the lifeboat and the oar of the organization during tough times. It is during these times that the leader's effectiveness will be most judged and will absolutely be most needed.

Call to Action

1. Can you find a way for your employees to have a sense of ownership?

2. Understand and accept that tough times are inevitable. Harden your personal and company core values before the storm ensues. List some actions that you can take to maintain your personal core values during the hard times. List some coaches and resources that can function as anchors during the most difficult times.

1

CHAPTER 10

THE COLLABORATIVE LEADER

Leaders don't force people to follow; they invite them on a journey.
—CHARLES S. LAUER, FORMER PUBLISHER
OF MODERN HEALTHCARE MAGAZINE

It's Not about You

THINK BEYOND YOURSELF AND YOUR OWN INTERESTS

When I was leading the company, I always had the team's best interests in mind first. Joni, the director of our HR department, once told me, "One thing I know about you is that every decision you make is in the best interest of this company."

I believe that to be true, that my decisions weren't necessarily best for my own personal interests. In retrospect, I now realize that they were in my personal best interest too—in the long term. Since I had significant interest in the company—my job, career, compensation, stock value—any decision I made was, by default, in my own best interest long term. However, on any given day, decisions that were made could not be about me—they had to be about what was in the best interest of the firm and the people of the firm.

It's not about you...

How You Treat Your People ...

I've seen leaders who can't wait to criticize or berate someone for a mistake, but that's not being a good mentor *or* leader. I've done it too. Remember the employee I talked about earlier, the young woman who was wonderfully talented but ultimately left the firm? I would argue that when that happens, leaders are thinking only about themselves. They're thinking, "Something that employee did is making me—the leader—look bad."

There is something more to life and to leadership than what makes you look good or brings personal gain at any given moment.

Leaders can reach their highest level of success if they realize it's *not* about them—it's about the people and the company as a whole. And if they approach decisions in that manner, then to a large degree, the business side will take care of itself.

People have to come first. If you get the people part right, all the rest—revenue, profit, sales, growth—will take care of itself.

GREAT LEADERS DON'T CARRY A CHIP ON THEIR SHOULDER

To anyone reading this book who grew up without a father, parental figure, or mentor, or anyone who was dealt a rotten hand in life—whatever that might be—my advice would be to accept it and move on. Great leaders don't carry a chip on their shoulder. They don't go around thinking they have to prove something to somebody. Leadership should not be an opportunity to exorcise (or exercise) your personal demons. It should not be a place to get even for past real or perceived grievances. In this event, you will be focused on yourself, and no one—not even you—will benefit. *You're not the only person in the world who was dealt a rotten hand, and you have to accept that for what it is if you want to be in a leadership role.* It's not going to get better by wallowing in it or by thinking life gave you a raw deal.

The sooner you can accept the trials and challenges you go through and look for the lessons to be learned, the sooner you will become a stronger and better person—and a better leader. **Remember that it's not about you; it's about achieving great things for the people around you.**

Leadership and Empathy

As I said in chapter 5, one of the things that has become clear to me is how important it is for leaders to have empathy. *It's critical for you, as a leader, to have a significant amount of empathy* and to be able to put yourself in other people's shoes. If you make business decisions without thinking at a deeper level about how those decisions are going to affect people, a sterile corporate environment will evolve. If you want to have a people-oriented culture in which your employees come to work inspired, motivated, and engaged, you're going to have to display empathy. If you don't have it, recognize that fact and surround yourself with people who do. It takes time and experience to become a good leader, and it has to start with understanding how others feel and what they want.

The difference between what many leaders do and what *great* leaders do to achieve a people-oriented culture is found in a combination of these characteristics: *empathy plus patience* versus *logic plus business process.*

Many leaders demonstrate either empathy and patience *or* logic and business process. But **a great leader has empathy and patience and balances it against logic and business process.** We all want and need results, but empathy is what people want to see. It inspires them to work hard and achieve results for you. No one wants to work for a person who does not understand or care about the challenges they face in their jobs or their personal lives.

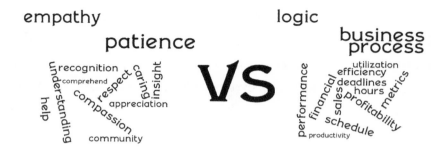

You must have both sides of the equation, but to me, empathy and patience win. Why? Because if you are in a service business, a "people" business, you will not be successful without them. You'll have minimal growth, and you'll see a revolving door, with employees constantly going in and out.

IT'S A BALANCING ACT: EMPATHY VERSUS BUSINESS

Good leaders have a genuine concern for others, and that's something you can't fake. However, I have often seen leaders present this genuine concern by consistently squabbling about raises for their team members, thinking workplace contentment is all about compensation. Sometimes leaders can't understand why their people aren't committed to work or why they won't do this or that, and they believe more compensation will cure employee issues. However, while commitment to people must be genuine, it should take on a holistic approach.

Money cannot compensate for the lack of strong relationships, career-growth opportunities, and a good workplace environment. Studies have shown that the number-one reason employees leave a job is due to a poor relationship with their boss—not money. Financial compensation must be competitive, but there comes a point of diminishing return for compensation if there is not a firm understanding that employee satisfaction is about more than just a paycheck. A recent McKinsey & Company article, "Money Can't Buy Your Employees' Loyalty," discusses how this idea has become even more true since the COVID-19 pandemic, as "organizations must evolve their paradigm by focusing on a holistic employee experience that puts equal emphasis on growth, engagement, and well-being."[4]

The same is true for life in general. Studies have shown that once people have enough money to cover basic human needs, clothes, schooling, shelter, food, the return on happiness is not strongly correlated with more money. Think also of parenting—a parent cannot buy long-term happiness for their child by working all the time and showering them with money at the cost of spending an inadequate amount of time with them. There are striking similarities in the relationship between the boss and his or her employees.

Empathy is something that psychologists and personality profilers will say you either have or you don't. I think that's mostly true. But I do think that life experiences can teach you to be aware of it and have an appreciation for it, as well as work to develop it. In either case, effective leaders need it or at least must have people around them who have it and can help the leader consider it in decision-making.

Empathy or an awareness of how to manage the lack thereof is also critical for success during times of crisis, when people are scared and unsure of the future. Of course, you have to make good business decisions that will protect the firm. However, you cannot do that without consideration for how those decisions will affect the people of the firm. *Your lack of empathy will show if you really only care about the bottom line, the business, or your own interests.* The trust people have in your leader-

---

4   McKinsey and Company, "Money Can't Buy Your Employees' Loyalty," published March 28, 2022, https://www.mckinsey.com/business-functions/ people-and-organizational-performance/our-insights/the-organization-blog/ money-cant-buy-your-employees-loyalty.

ship will erode, and it will be difficult, if not impossible, to overcome the impression you've made on people during that time.

HOW TO ALIENATE TALENTED PEOPLE

If decisions are based solely on logic and business process, you will alienate some very talented—and probably some of your best—people. More than likely, you'll even drive them out of the organization, and ironically, this will negatively affect that bottom line—which you are trying to protect!

If you have ever seen National Lampoon's *Christmas Vacation* from 1989, you may remember when Clark Griswold's boss, Mr. Shirley, decided to cut Christmas bonuses and instead gave the employees a jelly-of-the-month club membership. Cousin Eddie pointed out Mr. Shirley's blind spot to him by shackling, kidnapping, and taking him to the Griswold home to show him how what he had done affected the Griswolds. In response to having his blind spot fully illuminated, Mr. Shirley responds to Clark and his family by saying, "Sometimes things look good on paper but lose their luster when you see how it affects real folks ... It's people that make the difference."[5]

> *Great leaders aren't focused only on the bottom line.*
> *Great leaders understand the importance of*
> *the human side of their decisions and the*
> *importance of building consensus.*

With empathy driving part of their decision-making process, good leaders will also work toward consensus. That doesn't mean there won't

---

5   Chechik, Jeremiah, director. 1989. *National Lampoon's Christmas Vacation.* Warner Bros.

be tension in conversations, and, in fact, there should be. Consensus doesn't mean you will please everyone all the time. However, to get to the point where the opinions and voices of people are heard, some tension and debate are necessary to truly understand where people are coming from. All that should be considered when decisions are made. Only then can decisions be made that people will buy into and support, even when they don't totally agree with the final decision.

WHEN THERE IS NO BUY-IN OR CONSENSUS ...

As I said earlier, keep the current leaders and the next generation of leaders close to you. They can be your greatest cheerleaders or your harshest critics. Have frequent open discussions with them during the decision-making process.

WHEN LACK OF CONSENSUS HURTS ...

Years ago, we took a hard look at our healthcare costs and the associated plan and benefits. We had a traditional preferred provider organization (PPO) plan, and that was the only option for our employees. Health savings accounts (HSA) had become very popular and we determined that these plans would save a considerable amount in overall healthcare costs for both the company and the individual.

We proceeded to implement changes so that we could offer an HSA plan as well as a traditional healthcare plan option. We did not eliminate the traditional plan option immediately, because we wanted to give our employees time to understand the new plan and felt that, with time, all would come to understand the greater benefits of the HSA plan. I failed to discuss this process and get buy-in from everyone on our management team, the five-person team who led our entire company. Even though the HSA was clearly a better financial option for the company—and in almost all cases financially equal to or better for the individual—two members of the management team refused to opt for the HSA plan. Unfortunately, with those two members having their sphere of influence within the company, a clear message was heard by some within the organization that the management team was not on the same page, making it more difficult to get buy-in from the employees of the firm.

It took several years—much longer than we expected—before the two people on the management team finally opted for the HSA, and we were able to transfer most of the employees to the HSA plan. In fact, one of the management team members was one of the last employees to opt for the HSA. Again, I believe it was because I didn't do my due diligence in discussing it with them and working to get their buy-in and consensus—whether they totally agreed with it or not—before we implemented the plan. People want to be heard and know their ideas are taken into account.

THE CHALLENGES OF BUILDING CONSENSUS ...

After I scaled back my business activities to relax more and enjoy family time, I bought a boat. Seems like it would be a good thing, right? Of course it was, and what a blessing to be able to do that. But here comes the first-world problem—which I document to make a point about building consensus. I wanted everyone in the family to be happy and in agreement on which boat to buy, but I was torn between what some said they wanted and what I believed was practical. This turned into arguments, after which I felt guilty and unsettled. Now a really great blessing had become a stressor. I realized what I had done was try to make everybody happy. That doesn't work in your personal life; nor does it work in business. The best you can do is build consensus. Not everyone will agree, but hopefully they will understand and accept. Had I approached my family with more of a mindset of building consensus rather than trying to create universal happiness (whatever that is!), the boat situation would not have evolved into the guilt-producing, unsettling stressor that it was.

Decisions, Decisions, Decisions

GATHER DATA; SOLICIT INPUT. AVOID THE DANGERS OF *READY, FIRE, AIM* ...

I gather a lot of data when I make a decision. I solicit feedback from a lot of people to make what appears to be the right decision, all things considered—or at least a decision I can articulate and justify to everyone involved.

Sometimes I decide quickly after I feel I know all the salient facts around the issue. I act on it, make a decision to get it done, and move on—versus those who are prone to overanalyzing and making no decision. In my experience, I've found that, most of the time, even a bad decision is better than no decision or overanalyzing—as long as you have a good cause and can articulate why the decision was made.

> *If I waited until I had all my ducks in a row, I'd never*
> *get across the street. Sometimes you just have to gather*
> *up what you've got and make a run for it.*
> —JUDGE LYNN TOLER

But be careful: ***If you work in isolation, making all the decisions without understanding other people's points of view, it will be difficult, if not impossible, to get the buy-in needed to reach a high level of success in your company. Consensus is key.***

Thank goodness for people around me like Roman—one of my coaches—who often pushed back in times like these. He didn't hesitate to remind me that I needed to achieve consensus. He helped me slow down and listen to the people around me and incorporate their input.

MOVE FORWARD ...

Once the decision is made, don't look back or second-guess, but also don't stop listening to the people around you. Adjust if you need to. Learn from your mistakes, but ***don't let past mistakes stop you from moving forward.***

Putting It into Practice

STRATEGIC PLAN ...

I became president of the firm in 2013. One of the first things I did was travel to our offices and meet with lots of people, asking them questions such as, "Why did you come to work here? What keeps you here?" Based on what I heard at those meetings and several internal meetings afterward, we developed this strategic-plan graphic.

When we rolled out this document, we were saying that our people (employees) were the focus. That's what our culture was about: developing people and providing great service to clients. People had a lot of autonomy. You would also find a lot of teamwork, a high degree of integrity, and great quality work for our clients, some of whom told us we cared more about their projects than they did! At the core of it all, we were giving people the opportunity to grow in their careers. *Grow the company so people can grow*—this was the philosophy of our founder, Dr. Halff.

THE PROFIT MODEL ...

The question became, If we are all about people, why do we keep talking about profit? We developed the following profit model to connect the dots, so to speak, and show how it all fit together.

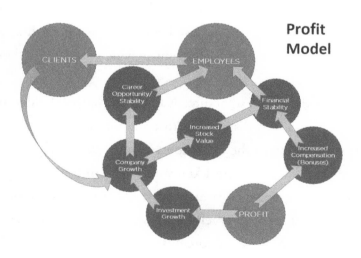

The concept was that all people come to work for financial reasons (to get paid) and for fulfillment in the job they do—with job fulfillment being the primary motivator. To that end, all profits were either invested in growth, creating career growth opportunities or paid to employees via compensation (bonuses).

> *Money simply satisfies basic needs. Job fulfillment satisfies something deeper and far more important to the individual.*

Increased profit leads to increased compensation for employees and increased stock value for everyone through the employee stock ownership plan. That satisfied everyone's basic need for financial stability.

The rest of the profit went to investment in growth for people (including training and development) and investments targeted for the growth of the company, which led to career opportunities for employees, thus satisfying the need for individual growth and job satisfaction. It created an environment in which people could say, "I am building a career here."

None of the profits went directly to owners or shareholders based on ownership. It was distributed to everyone based on merit and performance and what they were contributing. This is very unique—unlike almost any other firm I know of. Profits in firms are typically distributed to the owners (privately held) or to shareholders (publicly traded). This unique concept reinforces the principle that the company is about its people—first and foremost. What we do together is build the firm—not just me and what I do, not just a few owners at the top, and not just the shareholders that own stock.

Here are a few more thoughts about how this philosophy developed over the years:

If all employees are inspired, we will do great work for our clients. Clients will recognize that and give us more work, resulting in growth. That growth will drive career-growth opportunities and stock value growth, satisfying the personal and financial growth needs of the individual. Vaughn Aust, executive vice president of Integrated Solutions at MarketStar said it in a very simple way: "Happy employees lead to happy customers, which leads to more profits."

THE OWNERSHIP MODEL ...

Through a training program for our leaders, we also developed a leadership model that defined actions, values, and qualities that a person must possess to be an effective leader. We expanded the leadership model to say that it is really an ownership model and applies to everyone. It introduced the concept that ownership at every level—not only stock ownership, *but ownership in everything our people do*—is critical. Own it; be proud of it. If everyone has a strong sense of ownership in what they do, the people and the firm will be successful, and we will easily reach our goals.

These three tools—*the strategic plan, profit model, and ownership model*—became the cornerstone to drive the concept of a people-first culture; they provided a clear picture of the culture.

They helped to drive home what we were striving for:

- a stable workplace with career-growth opportunities for everyone

- a firm made up of inspired people who would provide great service for our clients

- a company where everyone had a sense of ownership and could be a shareholder in the firm

This resulted in a strong sense of ownership, which in turn resulted in financial stability for the firm, good compensation for everyone, and an atmosphere of teamwork.

It's about the success of the company, not just about the leader. If the company succeeds, I succeed. There's a term for this; it's called servant leadership, first introduced in an essay by Robert K. Greenleaf in 1970 and expanded upon in his 1977 book *Servant Leadership*. It defines the principle of serving other individuals and team members to foster growth. This is an authentic core value that must drive your actions as a leader, which will then and only then result in people behaving in this manner. Servant leadership simply means you're not driving the sled and screaming at the sled dogs, urging them to go faster. Instead, ***you are leading by serving***. A servant leader has made the decision to serve others to achieve teamwork, genuinely display empathy, and inspire collaboration.

Key Takeaways

- Great leaders understand the importance of collaboration. They understand the exponential power of the collective and demonstrate this in their actions—whether in risk assessment, profit initiatives, strategizing, or a multitude of other actions.

- Great leaders check their egos at the door and view their role as one more of service to the success of the organization as a whole.

Call to Action

1. How do your actions reflect an attitude of servitude?

2. Do any of your actions reflect emotional baggage from past pain? What actions can you take to keep personal baggage out of the workplace?

3. Get feedback from others to assess where your natural setpoint is on the spectrum from *ready, fire, aim* to *analysis paralysis*. Use this feedback to adjust your decision-making process (slow it down or speed it up).

CHAPTER 11

LIVING, LEADING, AND LEARNING THROUGH ADVERSITY

You don't know who you are until you've faced real adversity.
—DAN GASBY

What COVID-19 Taught Us

Americans used to be pretty indifferent to adversity when they saw it coming in the news, especially world events, because they assumed our country was so well prepared to handle it and protect us from it. With COVID-19, it was different. At first, I, along with many others, tended to think about it as another threat blown out of proportion while assuming nothing would come of it.

But then everything changed. First, there was disbelief when sporting events were canceled—the Final Four, the NBA, the start of baseball season. I thought then, "Maybe this is serious." But I was still skeptical. Then finally, more shutdowns made it real and extremely serious for all of us.

The pandemic caused tremendous grief and turmoil for millions of people. My heart goes out to those who lost loved ones, close friends, jobs, and businesses. While these have been truly difficult times, I feel also that some positives have come out of it for others, such as a new awareness of the fragility of life and the value of friends and family in our lives. Many people say the same thing. For others, the pandemic has totally disrupted lives in devastating ways. The point is that it impacted everyone differently; we must be aware of that fact going forward and empathetic to those who were severely affected by this crisis.

The pandemic was a black swan event that disrupted the world, shut down borders, and changed the way we live forever. I was fortunate from a business perspective, because our company was deemed an essential business. People could work; they could work from home because of robust IT systems that were in place. The transition from office to home went pretty seamlessly.

The negative was that I didn't have the face-to-face connection with close coworkers, friends, and extended family. I missed that. Our family did the best we could to connect, though; we got together for Easter via Zoom and played *Quiplash* together. We made some Zoom dates that were pretty special times. My wife set up Bible study with my daughter—every day!

Another negative has been watching some friends who struggled greatly with this virus. Some have dealt with and been treated for obsessive compulsive disorder (OCD) before COVID-19 came along. For years, they have worked on pushing back and dealing with the OCD symptoms of hurting (or in this case, infecting) someone, germaphobia, excessive handwashing and cleaning. Now suddenly, all that is validated! It has been absolute hell for people with OCD to deal with this challenge. They were fine with the stay-at-home sheltering, but the fear of "How do I stop the germs?" is overwhelming. It's no wonder we had toilet paper shortages at the beginning of this pandemic. There is no logic to it; it starts with a logical thought or action and snowballs into totally illogical and uncontrollable thoughts, actions, and reactions.

The point is that the pandemic affected people so differently. We will have to recognize and accept that people have been affected by this to varying degrees and accept that each individual's reentry into the workplace will be different. We will have to be flexible in how we deal with working from home versus coming to the office and how people need to cope with the effects of this pandemic in the future. The *Forbes* publication addresses this issue in the May 2022 edition entitled "Empathy Is Here to Stay: 3 Important Reasons It Will Shape the Future." In this article, the author outlines the impacts of the pandemic and the ensuing challenges to people's well-being. The author states that "empathy is here to stay because of the shared experiences and problems people have faced together." This collective experience produces the power of empathy, which "bodes well for a future of work in which people can express themselves fully and bring their best, because they are supported and experience a positive culture of empathy."[6]

Dealing with Adversity

The COVID-19 crisis created adversity that no one was prepared for. There will be disruptive events in the future but perhaps not of this magnitude. Who knows? But in any case, COVID-19 has forced many of us to simplify our lives.

---

6   Tracy Brower, "Empathy Is Here to Stay: 3 Important Reasons It Will Shape
      the Future," published May 8, 2022, https://www.forbes.com/sites/tracy-
      brower/2022/05/08/empathy-is-here-to-stay-3-important-reasons-it-will-shape-
      the-future/?sh=698590092cb6.

If I were to give one bit of advice for dealing with adversity, I'd say *prepare for adversity before the adversity hits.* If you have not prepared for it, it will be overwhelming, devastating, and very difficult to deal with. You will have emotional reactions based on fear and desperation.

One of the most important things we need when adversity hits is help from people around us—emotional, physical, or financial help. This preparation happens long before the adversity strikes—in how we treat the people around us. Why would anyone want to help you when you need help if you didn't show over time that you cared about them and were ready to help them if needed? Or you put them so far down on the priority list that you never had time for them?

> *Preparing for adversity means surrounding yourself with good people and showing that you care about them.*

Another piece of advice that many have learned through this crisis is to *create balance in your life.* Don't put all your eggs in one basket. Yes, work is important. But what happens when you can't do it anymore?

I wonder if perhaps I was fortunate to have the health issues a few years ago to help me fully understand how quickly you can lose things in life—and you have no control over that. *God didn't create you for your job only.* We all need to have more than just work in our lives! Make sure you maintain a strong family life. Stay young, at least in mind if you can't in body, and don't get old in spirit. No one wants to be around a curmudgeon. As noted, I was once called a curmudgeon and realized later it was a pretty accurate description for that time. If my wife and I were old, grumpy people, do you think we would have been invited to *Quiplash* games via Zoom with our millennial kids?

Keep your friends close. Make time for them. Have at least one, two, or three close friends. That means doing things with them and helping them when it's not convenient. I have a group of friends that I go fishing with once a year. The timing is rarely convenient. There are always other things in my life that are also important to me, and I could easily say no. But if I did that, those friends would not be friends for long. We, by default, would grow apart. I must choose to invest in those relationships!

None of this is rocket science. We all have heard it: "***God, family, and friends.***" What COVID-19 did was remind me just how important these are. Still, leaders of firms have a tendency to place work and career above all else. I don't think I have ever heard the saying, "Career, God, family, and friends." Why is that? Because life simply doesn't work well that way. Yet oftentimes this is what life becomes with leaders: work, work, and more work.

More crises will come along, perhaps not as devastating or worldwide, but they will come. And you will be much better prepared for it if you have diversity in your work and life and a circle of people who care about you and whom you care about. It's a two-way street.

The other aspect of preparing for crisis is the financial piece. Part of why I was able to weather this storm is because I am financially stable. The key for me was a lifelong approach to a life of ***living within my means. It's always important to work toward this goal.***

I don't have to have everything, don't have to have the best, and never lived paycheck to paycheck. I started with virtually nothing when I left home many years ago, but I was able to become financially stable because of my ability to save and not overspend. Living within one's means should be a way of life, because you never know when you might lose your job or savings. No, I never anticipated COVID-19; no one anticipated the Great Depression, 9/11, or the economic crash of 2008 either.

Spending less than you make, diversifying investments, having a rainy-day fund, ***developing multiple sources of income if you can***—all these are crucial to financial survival … and to your peace of mind during difficult times.

The bottom line is that it's paramount to ***set the stage before the adversity comes***. Then, when it does, you will be much better prepared to keep a logical head and avoid emotional reactions.

Take steps every day to keep the big picture in mind, but also take time to focus on the moment—why you are doing what you are doing on this day, in this moment. As my psychologist taught me, don't spend too much time thinking in the past or the future. Think about where you are today, what you will do now to reach a simple short-term goal—and that goal may be as simple as financial survival for this week.

What causes most anxiety is constantly thinking of the past (e.g., "I screwed up; I should have done this or that") or the future (fear of the unknown and of the worst possible outcome), not the present. And most of the time, the present is not that bad.

> *To be a leader in the most difficult times,*
> *you must have things you can always count on—*
> *these are your strongholds.*

There will be events in our lives that will be tragic. It was for many people with COVID-19. I haven't written much about spirituality yet. Someday *this* world will end for all of us. Many people have not come to grips with that. Our deep-brain chemistry is designed for protecting this body we have and staying alive in this world. That makes it very difficult to think about our own mortality. I can't tell you how to do this, but in the face of adversity, there must be some established spirituality. You have a mind, but you also have a spirit.

There is no way anyone can have all the answers to life, but *I find peace when I just step back and trust that it's all bigger than me.* There are lots of books on this subject and people to talk to who can help you figure this out for yourself. Your spiritual beliefs may be different from mine, and that's OK. To be a leader in the most difficult times, I would simply like to emphasize this: stay positive, continue to move forward, and have something you can have faith in and count on.

I believe that humans need a spiritual connection. And humans also need other humans.

Keep your friends and family close—always.

Key Takeaways

- Good leaders must understand that disruptive events are inevitable in both business and personal life. Many disruptive events are those that we wouldn't (or couldn't) have conceived of prior to their occurrence.

- Prepare both your personal and organization's financials for disruptive events.

- Build up your spiritual and emotional bank accounts before disruptive events occur.

Call to Action

1. What will be your strongholds during disruptive events?

2. What can you do to maintain these strongholds during good times?

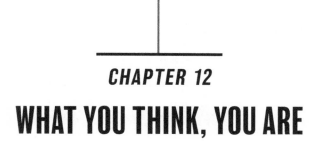

CHAPTER 12

WHAT YOU THINK, YOU ARE

Nothing can harm you as much as your own thoughts unguarded.
—THE BUDDHA

Self-Checkup

How often do we actually pay attention to the thoughts we have? Probably not often enough! They're silent, after all. ***Make sure you check on your own internal self-talk during your endeavors.***

You'll need to work on your thoughts if you're going to be a great leader. Half the battle is fighting the doubts in your head; then you've got to confidently inspire others.

When the going gets tough, be intentional and go through this thought process regarding whatever issue is at hand. Ask yourself, "What's the worst thing that can happen?" De-escalate the situation before you make a mountain out of a molehill. In addition, consider these other questions:

What is the best outcome possible?

What is the most likely thing that will happen?

Your answer to the last question is what you should take steps toward. Use coworkers, friends, and family to help.

FOCUS ON THE POSITIVES

Sometimes our thoughts are the most difficult things to control—so you need to focus on the positives as much as possible. ***There are ALWAYS positives if you look for them.*** The brain does not let us do that easily. The brain is naturally trying to protect this body of ours and is inclined to focus on the negative, to protect it. It's just the way humans are wired. It takes work to train yourself to think about the positives. Take time every day to do this in the morning when you get up, during the middle of the day, and at the end of the day before you go to bed. Discuss this with family and friends; tell them you are *not* OK with constantly talking about the negatives. Unfortunately, that probably means turning off the news most of the time.

> Sometimes our thoughts are the most difficult things to control—so you need to focus on the positives as much as possible.

While these words of advice are at the forefront of my mind because of the pandemic, I have worked hard to follow them all the time, not just when a crisis hits. If you practice the lessons I've laid out—maintaining strong relationships with family and friends, building financial stability, developing a spiritual life, and focusing on the positives—you will be much better prepared for the challenges that come along in your life. You might even be a happier person—even when challenges aren't there. But when they do come along, you'll be ready. Perhaps you received a difficult diagnosis. Maybe you endured the breakup of a valuable relationship. Perhaps you lost everything in the stock market or you have clients who canceled major contracts.

Regardless of what the crisis is, I can promise you that these lessons that I have learned work. You can follow them and get yourself into a good place to cope with crisis.

Life's challenges, and the stress that comes with them, affect our loved ones too. I saw how the pandemic impacted family and friends. That impacted me, too, because it saddens me to see them stressed, depressed, and anxious. The best advice I can give is to work with those around you to help shift a negative thought process or help find them other resources to facilitate this. Identifying the positive and focusing on the positive things happening in their lives—even through adversity—can initiate healing. There is no question my past physical and mental challenges impacted my wife. I could see it. Kathy wasn't in the same place I was, but I think it was often harder on her than it was on me. She saw a loved one in pain and anguish but struggled to know how best to help. ***Remember that when bad things happen to you, you're not in it alone.*** It hurts the ones around you just as much—maybe more than it hurts you.

You will survive the event of the day. As my doctor once told me in biblical tones: "This, too, shall pass." (And as a saying—source unknown—I once read said, "Yes, it may pass like a kidney stone, but it will indeed pass.") And yes, someday that moment will come, and we won't survive physically. Have the faith and courage to understand that when that day comes, it is God's will for us to leave this world. We can't completely control the world around us, and we must stay grounded in our understanding that sometimes what is meant to be is *meant to be.* Once we come to terms with that, much of the anxiety and fear subsides and allows us to think more clearly, cope with the challenges in life, and move forward.

Forget about the Other Guy

Whether you're an executive or entrepreneur, starting your first job, or a college student, you'll always face doubt and skepticism. Oftentimes that exists primarily in your own mind. Comparison can be a killer and the enemy of your success. There's always someone better than you—or, at least, perceived to be better.

For me, it was Bob—supposedly the smartest guy in class (more like the smartest jerk in the class). I got out of college and started work, but there was always someone who was ahead of me. And it didn't seem like they should be. They were praised when they shouldn't have been, had their own businesses—perceived to be successful. Often, they were real jerks, kind of like Bob. But what goes around comes around; your success is not determined by their success or failure. Focus instead on what your journey is meant to be.

> *Comparison can be a killer and the enemy of your success.*

People ultimately succeed or not; firms come and go. Leaders make money and often sell their firm, but what about everyone else who made the money for them? What happens to those leaders who never cared about those people who made contributions along the way, whether great or small? Stick to your values; rewards will come. Don't worry about how much the *other* guy makes, a friend of mine, Bill, once told me.

IT WON'T ALWAYS BE FAIR

Sometimes I thought I was better and deserved more than the recognition and compensation I received; I probably wasn't and probably didn't. But that's what you'll encounter in your leadership journey and in life. It won't always be fair, and when it isn't, you'll learn some pretty good lessons. *Leaders are important, but great teams are essential*—and it all starts with mindset.

It takes time to build a great team. You can't do that with a negative mindset, and you can't do that by expending energy on worrying about the other guy—or how fair or unfair the world around you is.

Talk the Talk ... Walk the Walk

People are watching your every move. It's not just what you say; it's what you do—maybe even more so.

ACTIONS SPEAK LOUDER THAN WORDS

The people-first culture started with one of the greatest influencers in my life, Dr. Halff. He started the company from nothing and always said he wanted it to be the greatest company in the world.

Yes, the world!

He truly believed that to create that, he needed to reward the next generation of leaders. And he lived those words.

Testimony to that fact could be seen when he sold the firm. He sold it to the next generation of leaders at book value. Book value is about a third of what he could have sold it for on the open market. And he did it with financing so we could pay for it out of profits, without much angst or pressure, after he stepped down. That says it all. It solidified the culture and told his successors who he was and what he believed in. That culture has stood the test of time— more than thirty years and three generations of leadership later, the company is now a firm of well over a thousand people.

We built a culture of teamwork and ownership. One of the most critical times in building that culture came during the 2008 economic downturn—those days tested us and tested our core values. I told our leaders, "How we handle this downturn and treat one another will define who we are and what we are made of—individually and as a firm. It will challenge our culture. It will become our culture." How in the world did I know that back then? Was I guessing? Was I lucky? Was it divine intervention? Was it instinct? I think some of it was instinct and *a lot of what I learned from Dr. Halff.*

> **Learn from others.**
> **Crises will test you on all levels.**

We made it through the downturn of 2008 and the pandemic of 2020. We did it together. We all learned many lessons in the 2008 era. The trust and sense of true teamwork between individuals were built during that downturn. And I believe the same will hold true as we turn the corner on the pandemic of 2020.

Don't discount the advice and thoughts of those who have gone before you. Some of their ideas may be out of date, but the basic values they developed and the experiences they lived through have merit. They learned some important things; there is much to learn from them—and it's much easier than learning the hard way.

INSTINCTS—ARE THEY NATURAL OR ARE THEY LEARNED?

Our director of human resources, Joni, told me I had good instincts with people. Can that be taught? I don't really think so—it's more of an evolutionary process. I think it's all about your values, passion, courage, and conviction to stick to your values, no matter what. It's also about learning from your mistakes and experiences—and from others. I am not the same person I was twenty years ago. It's amazing how my instincts have improved now that I have so many more life experiences. Surround yourself with good people who can recognize your weaknesses. People who have the courage to challenge you will help you with your blind spots.

BUILDING THE FIRM; DOING THE HARD THINGS THAT HAVE TO BE DONE ...

Building is an important part of leadership. To be able to do that, you will have to do some difficult things. You'll have to recognize problems and deal with them. The culture of teamwork and ownership didn't always exist throughout the firm like it does today. It took many years of hard work, addressing challenging issues. There was infighting between teams. Teams didn't all trust one another. Some of those leaders did not and would not *ever* fit the culture Dr. Halff started—the culture that I and others embraced.

CULTURAL INCOMPATIBILITY ...

There was one team leader, who was a good friend of mine, who failed to embrace the culture. I knew him and his wife well. We partied together and watched football games together. But he was a liar—a pathological liar. He lied when he didn't need to. He was all about himself, not the team, not the firm. Everybody knew it. I finally had to let him go, and it was agonizing to do that to a friend. But this decisive action set the stage for a stronger culture, because it sent the message to employees that this behavior would not be tolerated. It wasn't easy, because he brought a lot of work in the door and made good money for the firm. But at the end of the day, for the sake of his team and the firm—and most importantly for the culture of the firm and what we were trying to build—it had to be done.

Some of the things we have to do as leaders are hard, unpleasant, and uncomfortable, and often those who don't sit in your chair won't understand. They will think you are a heartless business executive who doesn't care about the people of the firm. But that couldn't be further from the truth. ***It is, in fact,* because *of the people of the firm that sometimes hard decisions have to be made*** and distasteful courses of action need to be carried out.

You have to be careful about deciding when to let an employee go or when to keep them. The repercussions of letting people go will be felt throughout the team and maybe even the entire firm. Most people have friends at the firm. No one likes to see their friends being shown the door. It has to be done with respect, in a way that people—even their friends—will understand that it was the right thing to do—if you want a people-first culture, that is.

How do you make that decision? When deciding to let someone go who is not a cultural fit, ***you have to balance revenue, profit, and***

the morale of the rest of the staff. You have to stay in control (as much as possible) and avoid letting your emotions enter the picture. Stick to your core values. This is when it is most important that your core values align with the core values you have articulated to the people of the firm—that culture you are working to create. This, too, is when everyone will be watching and taking note. Do you practice what you preach? Or preach and then practice something else?

You absolutely must put the right people in the right seats on the bus. However, just because people are not doing well does not necessarily mean they need to be let go. Maybe they are in the wrong seat, or maybe you haven't given them the tools to succeed. Or, in the case above, they may not fit. Some may never fit the culture, and you'll need to do what you have to do.

> **"All we did was try to put people in the right seat and then just let them run."**

Roman, my longtime coworker and friend, stepped down from his position as chief operating officer at the same time I stepped down from being president. This is what he said during our last message to the entire company: "We didn't really do anything; all we did was try to put people in the right seat and then just let them run." He was exactly right.

DEALING WITH THE DIFFICULT PEOPLE ...

Some say most people are bad, mean, ill-willed, difficult—you choose a word. I would say most people are good at the core. They become difficult when you can't figure out how to work with them—or communicate with them. There is no level of trust. And then those people occupy all your time and energy. You don't spend time and energy on the "good" people, because you don't need to! That leads you to be consumed by the difficult people and results in the notion that most people are difficult. If you really think that, then the first person to look at is yourself.

KEEP YOUR EMOTIONS IN CHECK ...

One day, when I was chief operating officer—in one of the finer moments for both of us—my former boss came to see me and gave me a colorful lecture on how I was screwing up. Over a minor printer problem. I, of course, provided an equally colorful response. He told me that he deserved respect. I bit right back, explaining that to get respect one has to earn it. After the heated exchange, I internalized the events, let them eat at me. I went back to visit with him a couple of days later to try to clear the air. The exchange was much calmer, but he told me that I was *all* of the problem, to which I stated maybe he should look in the mirror. After reflecting on this more, I realized he was partially right. I *was* part of the problem. The heated exchanges over time had caused me to allow my emotions to get the best of me. It had gotten to the point that if he said something was black, I would say it was white—no matter what. With my emotions controlling me, I immediately decided he was wrong and that he was the bad guy. But he was *not* the bad guy. I had just lost the desire and ability to try to communicate with him. Look at yourself in the mirror. Someone needs to keep telling you that. Someone needs to see and point out your blind spots.

> *Find a way to look in the mirror. Get yourself a coach, some mentors! Iron sharpens iron.*

Key Takeaways

- Watch the self-talk—you can be your own best friend or your own worst enemy.

- Put effort into focusing on the positive. The negative will come naturally because it's instinctive—the positive is not! This includes not forgetting to recognize the work of the "good, nondisruptive people" of the organization because your energies are soaked up by the "disruptive people."

- Focus on what *your* journey is **meant to be**, not what the journey of *others* **is.** When we focus on the *uniqueness of our journey*, stress and anxiety dissipate.

Call to Action

1. Take yourself in for an emotional checkup periodically by asking yourself the tough questions and by getting feedback from others.

2. What difficult tasks will be required of you in your role as a leader? How can you frame these roles in your self-talk to understand their importance and not let it affect your self-esteem? For example,

   "I have to let this employee go—it will affect them and their family in a negative way. However, I will be providing for the well-being of all the employees of my company by maintaining a financially stable organization."

   Or in some cases, the internal dialogue may look something like this:

   "I have to let this employee go—it will affect him and his family in a negative way. However, this organization is not a good fit for this employee—by keeping him, he will affect his coworkers negatively, and it may inhibit him from finding a place better suited to his passion and his personal growth."

CHAPTER 13

THE NEXT SCENE

Leadership is about making others better as a result of your presence and making sure that impact lasts in your absence.
—SHERYL SANDBERG, COO OF FACEBOOK

Find Your Successor

It took a long time to develop a people-first culture at our firm, but we got there. So the question becomes, **How do you keep that culture going?**

From the moment I became president, I told myself, "I am going to find my successor and leave this place in better shape than it was!"

Find people and mentor them so that when the day comes for you to step down, you are confident that you can do it and be at peace with your decision. This isn't a quick and easy process, but it's essential if you are committed to your business and your people. **Don't wait; start working on your successor now.**

There comes a point when you have to let it go, whether that's to step down from your current position or move up to the next level. Sometimes that decision gets made for you, but if you are in the top leadership position, more than likely you will have to make that decision yourself.

It's hard to let go. As a leader, you give your opinions and ideas of what needs to be done—and because you have been successful, you have confidence in yourself and think no one else can do your job effectively. But when you move on to that next position or step down from your position of leadership, you have to let it go. **Let people do their jobs and use their own skills, talents, and passion to get things done.**

You know they won't do it as well as you did (or so you think), and you will have the tendency to second-guess and see the "wrong" in the way they do things. You know they will make mistakes, but remember, you have to let it go.

Transition

When I stepped down as president, I spent a lot of time thinking about what I did right ... and what I did wrong. Was I successful? I tried to understand what success really meant after leading a company for decades, asking myself if it was worth it.

It was honestly an adjustment to stop, reflect, and get comfortable with who I am. It was a little scary at first, but **once I came to grips with stepping away, the fear was replaced with excitement for what the future holds**. During those first couple of weeks when I stepped away as president, it created a huge sense of relief, a shift in how I viewed life. You tap into a real positive sense of accomplishment when you make these kinds of decisions. You also see how it affects other people in your life.

> Let people do their jobs and use their own skills, talents, and passion to get things done.

My family saw a change in how I lived. There's a season for everything, and the one I'm in now includes more peace, quiet, and relaxation. When I left my position, I felt the weight of the world had been lifted off my shoulders. I found out that stepping down from a position of leadership—where you ultimately make a lot of the final decisions—can be absolutely great. You can literally feel the stress that comes with those decisions leaving your inner self. It's a tremendous feeling of relief, and it's great to not be worrying about fifty-six million things all at once.

However, I also found that letting go can be very difficult. You have been in a position where your voice is heard, you have significant influence, and then one day your opinion doesn't matter anymore. It's almost like letting go of your child. You have invested so much time and energy in building and growing something special—but then you need to let it go.

HOW DO YOU MAKE THAT DECISION?

Everything you do, your whole sense of self-worth, can be tied to the things you do as the leader. How do you get to the point where you know it's time to let go?

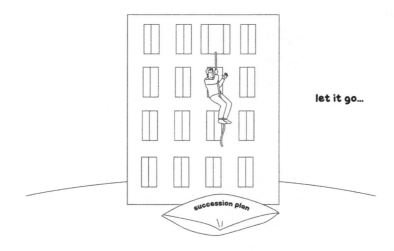

Personally, I began to think back to when my dad died.

Fathers influence their children's lives greatly. Their absence, or presence, changes you forever. When my father passed away at forty-six, I was only six. This idea has always lingered in the back of my mind: "How long am I going to live?" I never realized how much it affected me to have a father who died when I was so young. No child knows how to process that. Over time, I came to see how his absence affected me; in many ways, it was a very positive thing. It drove me to never let anyone or anything knock me down. But in some ways, it hurt me. His passing caused me to be too driven and left me with a chronic sense of insecurity. There was a voice in my head telling me, "Nothing is enough to be secure in life. Don't ever stop working hard, because you are alone in this world and no one is there to help you but yourself. You don't have time to stop and enjoy life."

But now I tell myself to slow down, enjoy life, and smell the roses. My wife laughs, because I told her years ago that I wanted to retire at forty-six, the age my dad was when he passed away. There's a context of past (learning from change), present (being the change), and future (accepting change). That was always in the back of my mind. My dad died when he was young, so how long will I live? There are things I want to do, things I want to enjoy. And then, the unexpected health issues drove the point home.

I can't tell you exactly how to make the decision as to when it's time to transition, but what I can tell you is this: Don't wait to enjoy life until it's too late—or until some traumatic event happens in your life. Think it through now. Just like in business, develop a plan: a plan to enjoy life, a transition plan for when the time is right for you. And follow up with that plan just like you would with anything else that's important to you.

AVOIDING THE DEEP VOID ...

Nobody knows how long they will live. At some point, you need to just enjoy life. No, I don't want to work until I'm seventy or eighty, because I have seen too many in this situation affected by poor health.

I tell myself I want to enjoy my life—now. But it took some pretty traumatic events in my life to get there. Those difficult times caused me to think at a deeper level about who I am and why I do the things I do.

> **Don't wait to enjoy life until it's too late.**

The transition out of leadership was challenging, and it taught me a few things. As a leader, you go home each night thinking you did something significant. What is going to replace that feeling? All of a sudden, your voice isn't needed—maybe not even wanted. Your influence is gone, and there is a deep void.

It can be quite challenging to figure out what life was about. What was the thing that inspired you? What gave you a reason to get up in the morning? It can be hollow. *It helps if you can say that you accomplished something important and meaningful for yourself.*

I found, after a lot of soul searching, that over time I helped navigate people through a lot of positive transition. When I became chief operating officer, the culture that Dr. Halff had strived for had eroded. Leaders often didn't trust each other, didn't like each other, and quite frankly, in some cases, were highly dysfunctional. This dysfunction created an environment in which some leaders were rogue players and did their own thing. Sometimes this benefited the company, but many times they were just serving their own self-interests. They covered it up pretty well. I worked for many years to change that and to rebuild a people-oriented culture. But I absolutely did not do it by myself. Many other leaders who believed in the company and in the legacy of Dr. Halff contributed greatly. I realize now that I was committed to making the firm a better place to work, one in which leaders trusted in themselves and each other and where they worked well together.

I worked to build consensus among the good people at the firm by facilitating difficult conversations that were absolutely necessary. Those conversations created an environment in which ***people felt heard, and it built trust*** so that people could play well together in the same sandbox. In retrospect, I can see that I spent most of my time talking to people, building trust, creating consensus, and bringing people together for a common good, all while meeting the individual's goals, needs, and wants.

I believe that's what it takes if you want to create a people-oriented culture where people believe in the purpose and direction of the company. ***You have to take time to have lots of one-on-one conversations. Build trust in each other and a consensus that the direction you and the company are heading, and the culture you are creating, will bring rewards for everyone***—financial and personal-growth rewards. I feel like I had a hand in making the company a better place to work. Reflection on that achievement of putting people first is what brings me the greatest sense of reward, the greatest sense of accomplishment. I helped make it a place that has a people-first culture, where people had the opportunity to grow in their careers. They were able to chase and accomplish their own dreams and goals. That is how I find peace and can honestly say I believe I was successful.

MAKING A SEAMLESS TRANSITION ...

I believe that self-reflection is important for every leader. Otherwise, if we never evaluate why we do what we do, at some point, we could wake up feeling pretty hollow and unfulfilled. Leaders who are driven by power and control—or whose sense of identity is wrapped up in the company—may never understand what was really the most important to them during their careers. They will have a harder time celebrating when it is time to step down to let the next leaders lead; or worse, they may never have a chance to step down—to stop and enjoy the fruits of their labor.

> **Think now about what really drives you, what's most important to you.**

I stepped down from president about a year before I began writing this book. I feel that I have done much to put the company in a good place, one in which the next generation of leaders can succeed.

That transition has to be seamless for the company to be successful, and *that takes years of planning and execution.*

I am fortunate that I had some things happen that caused me to think about what drives me along the way. Don't wait for things to happen to you to do that!

It's really easy when you step beyond the leadership position you are in today to second-guess and criticize those next leaders for the decisions they make. But you must transfer the role, support them in every way, and trust that they'll bring their best qualities to the job.

Your legacy is yours. Let them create theirs.

Key Takeaways

- It is often said that the job of every parent is to work themselves out of a job. This is just as true in business leadership.

- When it's time for you to step down, the transition should be as seamless as possible. Preparation should begin long before the transition.

- Just as your journey was unique to you, so will your legacy be.

- Letting go will be easier if you can reflect on your journey and realize that you accomplished something important and *meaningful* for yourself, as well as for others.

Call to Action

1. What do you want your legacy to be?

2. What similarities will your legacy have to your predecessors? What differences will it have?

3. Will you have the right successors in place who allow you to effectively work yourself out of your leadership role?

EPILOGUE

I am fully retired now. After a fulfilling career, it feels good to be retired and to be able to do the things I enjoy without the stress or tension that goes along with the responsibilities of being in a leadership position. For years I had the pleasure of working with some tremendously brilliant, great people, and together we created a unique people-first culture. The closure in my career came at a retirement event that was so graciously planned and provided by the leaders of the firm, for me and for my career-long coworker and friend, Roman, who retired three months after I did. This event helped me to realize that, in the end, *it was all worth it.* Many of my colleagues, coworkers, and friends were there, many of whom I had hired, whom I had worked with for many years, whom I had trained and mentored—and who taught me many of the lessons that I learned along the way that I shared in this book. To see all those people in one place one more time and to realize that they were working toward those same goals of the firm that Dr. Halff started—working to build and grow a firm, to give the employees of the firm the opportunity to grow and prosper—and to be able to call the people in that room my friends gives me great pleasure and the ability to say that *yes, I was successful.*

A COMPENDIUM OF LEADERSHIP LESSONS LEARNED

At the end of the day, it's *all about people*. From Zig Ziglar: "You don't build a business. You build people, and people build the business."

Define your long-term vision through strategic planning. Whatever your goals are, you must be personally, honestly passionate about the goal and vision for where the firm is headed. Strategic planning is about bringing everyone together to define common ground regarding the goals of the company. That way, everyone sees where they fit in and how they can personally benefit if the firm reaches its goals and vision.

Transparency on the part of employers helps build a greater sense of ownership in people. The greater the sense of ownership, the more fulfilled people will be in their jobs and careers and the more successful the company will be.

People need to be *inspired*, not motivated. You can't motivate people. People motivate themselves.

If people are engaged and have a sense of ownership, they will come to work for something more than a paycheck. What people do at work must satisfy a personal need for them.

For people to find long-term happiness with their jobs, they have to come to work for something more than a paycheck. Money becomes secondary.

People need to see it's about the company's greater good to achieve great success. And that success has to satisfy a personal need for people, and it must inspire them. That's the trick ... to be able to articulate the vision of the company so it satisfies a need in people and inspires *everyone*. Again: People cannot *be* motivated. People motivate themselves.

How is winning defined for the firm? If every person sees the greater good and is inspired because of that, the firm will provide great service to its clients. Everything else will take care of itself, such as profits, workload, growth, and company goals. At that point, who cares what the competition is doing?

If you share the wealth using profit distribution, bonuses, or even by allowing people to have a piece of the pie through ownership, you (as owner) will be repaid many times over in the success of the company. You'll see an overall increase in profits and stock price, not to mention people growing professionally and personally.

How do you (the individual) define success? Being CEO? Reaching a certain level of financial wealth? These things alone will not do it. There has to be something more, something deeper. For me, that was seeing and helping people grow. Otherwise, when you reach these levels, you will be disappointed, disillusioned.

You are not made of steel. When something devastating happens, will you be able to be at peace? Happy? Asking yourself, Was it all worth it? It may not happen until you are sixty, seventy, or eighty, but it will happen. Ask anyone who has reached that age.

Is your journey really about personal happiness? Helping others, maybe? What good is all the money in the world, or being the king of the world, if you don't have others to share it with? Where does that come from? Helping others? Something spiritual? Be intentional about thinking on these things.

FOUNDATIONAL POINTS FOR LEADERSHIP SUCCESS

- People are the answer to everything.

- What drives you deep down is what will be revealed when you are under the most stress.

- "Correct" decisions are not always the best decisions.

- We all have blind spots. I have mine. You have yours.

- Find someone to help you. Don't wait until it's too late.

- Many executives are unaware when they're in burnout mode.

- In today's world, it seems that overwhelming stress is the rule, not the exception. Take a break to deal with it.

- Find a way to live in the moment.

- Fears and worst-case-scenario thinking can become the catalysts for visionary thinking.

- The overarching goal: growth—to create opportunities and financial rewards for all.

- Plan ahead to develop leaders in the company.

- Look at the person before letting them go. Ask these questions: Are they in the right seat? Are we giving them the tools to succeed?

- People want to feel heard, listened to, and appreciated!

- When things go wrong, most of the time we all have some culpability.

- People become engaged and a deep level of trust and loyalty evolves when leaders have empathy and truly understand and care about the challenges their employees face.

- You will survive if you don't lose sight of your overall vision and values.

- Leaders need coaches.

- You get to decide whether the challenges and changes you face will be a good thing or a bad thing.

- If it's not ultimately getting you closer to the primary objective, then why are you spending time on it?

- Never look back after your decision is made. It's a new day.

- If you can't tell people the why of decision-making, they will lose confidence in you as a leader. Effective leaders must have frequent open communication about decisions being made.

- Define your vision ... articulate it ... communicate it—consistently.

- Articulate how profit and growth goals benefit all employees.

- The actions you take in the difficult moments are what everyone will see and remember.

- People have to come first. If you get the people part right, all the rest—revenue, profit, sales, growth—will take care of itself.

- Great leaders aren't focused only on the bottom line. Great leaders understand the importance of the human side of their decisions and the importance of building consensus.

- Money simply satisfies basic needs. Job fulfillment satisfies something deeper and far more important for the individual.

- Preparing for adversity means surrounding yourself with good people and showing that you care about them.

- To be a leader in the most difficult times, you must have things to count on—these are your strongholds.

- Focus on the positives.

- Comparison can be a killer and the enemy of your success.

- Learn from others. Crises will test you on all levels.

- "All we did was try to put people in the right seat and then just let them run."

- Find a way to look in the mirror. Get yourself a coach, some mentors!

- Iron sharpens iron.

- Don't wait to enjoy life until it's too late.

- Think now about what really drives you, what's most important to you.

FAVORITE BOOKS

The Four Obsessions of an Extraordinary Executive by Patrick Lencioni

The Five Dysfunctions of a Team by Patrick Lencioni

The Shack by William P. Young

Strategy and the Fat Smoker by David Maister